Buying a Property in
Spain

Practical Books that inspire

Living and Working in Spain
The complete guide to a successful short or long-term stay

Living and Working in Portugal
Staying in Portugal – all you need to know

Retire Abroad
Your guide to a full and happy retirement in a foreign country

Getting a Job Abroad
The handbook for the international jobseeker

Buying a Property in France
An insider guide to finding your ideal house

Buying a Property in
Spain

*An insider guide to finding a
home in the sun*

HARRY KING

howtobooks

Published in 2002 by
How To Books Ltd, 3 Newtec Place,
Magdalen Road, Oxford, OX4 1RE, United Kingdom.
Tel: (01865) 793806. Fax: (01865) 248780.
email: info@howtobooks.co.uk
www.howtobooks.co.uk

First edition 2002
Reprinted 2002 (twice)
Reprinted 2003

British Library Cataloguing in Publication Data
A catalogue record for this book is available from
the British Library.

Cover design by Baseline Arts Ltd, Oxford

Produced for How To Books by Deer Park Productions
Edited by Diana Brueton
Typeset by Anneset, Weston-super-Mare, North Somerset
Printed and bound by Cromwell Press, Trowbridge, Wiltshire

NOTE: The material contained in this book is set out in good
faith for general guidance and no liability can be accepted
for loss or expense incurred as a result of relying in particular
circumstances on statements made in the book. The laws and
regulations are complex and liable to change, and readers should
check the current position with the relevant authorities before
making personal arrangements.

Contents

List of illustrations   10
Preface   11
Acknowledgements   13

1.   Introducing Spain   **15**
A dream that can come true   15
Common perceptions   16
Looking at the pros and cons of living in Spain   18
A picture of the country   23
Demographics   27
Summary   29

2.   Narrowing the Options   **30**
Planning to go   30
Deciding where to go   31
Green northern Spain   33
Diverse eastern Spain   34
Andalusia – southern Spain   38
Vast central Spain   42
The holiday islands   44
Summary   45

3.   Making a Start   **47**
Reading newspapers   47
Going to property exhibitions   48
Viewing alternatives   50
The international company   51
Estate agents   52
The Spanish estate agent – inmobiliaria   52
Viewing over the web   53
Understanding advertisements   54
Summary   55

4.	**What and Where to Buy**	**57**
	House names and their description	57
	The building specification	58
	Considering the pros and cons of each house type	59
	Living in urbanisations and communities	62
	New or resale?	64
	Living by the sea or in the country	64
	Which direction?	65
	Optional extras	66
	The magic housing ingredient – position	67
	Case study – purchasing	68
	What do people buy?	69
	Summary	70
5.	**The People Involved**	**71**
	The builder	71
	The agent	73
	The *abogado* (solicitor)	77
	The bank manager	79
	Case study – opening a bank account	83
	The *notario*	83
	The *gestor*	85
	Checking debts	85
	Avoiding problems	86
	The golden rules	87
	Summary	88
6.	**Understanding the Legal Documents for a New Property**	**89**
	Eleven important steps	89
	A plan of the house	91
	Locating the plot	91
	Reservation contract	91
	The *nota simple*	93
	The all important purchase contract	94
	Community charges – a share of the costs	95
	The *Certificado Final de la Direccion de la Obra*	96
	The *Licencia de Primera Ocupacion*	96
	Insurances	96
	The *escritura*	97
	Registro de la Propiedad	98

Small building alterations	98
Case study – purchasing a property with a mortgage	99
Summary	100

7. Money Matters — **101**
Property prices	101
A national picture	102
Paying the money	102
Allowing for additional buying costs	103
The black economy and black money	106
More capital costs?	107
What are the annual running costs of a Spanish home?	108
Summary	109

8. Before You Go — **110**
Learning the language	110
Case study – a typical language lesson	111
Taking your pets	112
Letting the house back home	113
Moving your furniture	114
Organising your travel	115
E-commerce	116
Summary	116

9. Linking It All Together — **117**
Moving in	117
Viewing the new property for the first time	118
Revisiting the *abogado*	119
Revisiting the bank	121
Case study – don't get mugged	122
The final payment	122
Going to the notary	123
Equipping the home	124
Summary	124

10. Buying Other Properties — **125**
Fast track conveyancing for new houses	125
Case study – paying the builder	129
Resale houses	129
Renovated or reformed houses	131
Building your own home	133

Town planning 134
Renovated and resale – good and bad contracts 136
Only one *abogado* 138
Summary 138

11. **Timeshare and Rental** **139**
Timeshare is changing 139
Looking at the property rental market 140
Holiday rental 140
Long term rental 142
Landlord's costs 143
Summary 143

12. **Cutting Red Tape** **144**
You or the *gestor*? 144
During the property purchase 144
Visiting the town hall 146
Applying for *residencia* 147
Meeting motoring regulations 147
Entering the Spanish health system 150
Making a will 150
Summary 151

13. **Dealing with your Finances** **152**
A personal life plan 152
Planning your pensions 153
Planning your investments 153
Investing in Spain 154
Dealing with personal taxation 155
Income tax 157
Capital gains 158
Wealth tax 159
Inheritance tax 159
Summary 161

14. **Learning about Culture** **162**
What is culture? 162
Es bueno descansar y no hacer nada despues! 162
Religion 163
The family group 163
How the Spanish party 164

Eating out 166
Customs, the arts and opera 167
The shopping experience 168
Buying wine and olive oil 172
Summary 174

15. **Living Life to the Full** **175**
Motoring 175
Dealing with the post 178
Getting the name and address correct 179
Coming to terms with communications 180
Three police forces 182
How foreigners party 182
El tiempo libre 183
Joining a social club 187
Summary 188

16. **Avoiding Failure** **189**
A need to learn 189
Case study – employment 189
Reasons for failure 190
Summary 192

Appendices
1. A purchase contract issued by a builder for a
new property **193**
2. The community rules 199
3. The *escritura* 205
4. A purchase contract drawn up by an *abogado* 212
5. An option contract signed on behalf of a
client by an agent 215
6. The communities of Spain and their provinces 217
7. Public holidays 220
8. English language newspapers 221
9. Useful addresses 222
10. Further reading 224
11. Common questions 226
12. Useful phrases 228

Index 233

List of Illustrations

1. A map of Spain   14
2. Recent history   25
3. Statistics   32
4. The viewing choice   49
5. Plan – A terraced property   60
6. Plan – Two bedroom corner bungalow   61
7. Plan – Two floor detached property with a solarium   61
8. Buying considerations   63
9. *Los hombres grandes* of the buying process   72
10. The most important legal documents   90
11 Architect's drawing   92
12. Different purchasing procedures   126
13. The importance of the town hall   131
14. Red tape decision tree – non residents – holiday
    home   145
15. Red tape decision tree – new residents   145
16. European taxation levels   156
17. A typical menu   167
18. Traditional Spanish culture   168
19. Culture of the new residents   183
20. What expatriate Brits miss most   184

Preface

Today's Spain is a young vibrant country barely three decades old, but no land is so diverse and enjoys such an excellent climate. It has a strong personality, is full of rich traditions, has a different culture and a proud history.

Tourism has changed the face of Spain for ever. Fishing villages have been replaced with skyscraper hotel blocks. Artificial flamenco, staged bullfights and tacky souvenirs are the entertainment for visitors. Yet only a few kilometres inland, villages, towns and cities lie untouched and retaining their own distinctive way of life.

Spain has a rapidly expanding economy reaping the benefits of membership of the EU. Major international companies are investing in the country against a background of stable political government and a multilingual labour force. Yet the old links to agriculture still exist. Orange and lemon groves, flowering almond trees, thousands of acres of vines and millions of olive trees still remain.

Property is not expensive. It is quite different and the choice is great. White houses in distinctive styles are built in urbanisations or scattered on hillsides for use as holiday homes or for permanent residence. Buyers want homes to enjoy for themselves and their families. They are not property speculators.

The buying procedures are also very different. Forget the traditional approach of putting in an 'offer', arranging a mortgage and asking your solicitor to sort things out. Prospective buyers must carry out research and ask questions themselves, rather than assuming a solicitor will deal with these matters. Learn about the *abogado*, the *notary*, the *gestor*, the contract and the *escritura*. It will make things so much easier. It is necessary to understand the Spanish conveyancing system from start to finish. It can trap the unwary in a country where there are many property horror stories.

A new property buyer will to a degree always remain a foreigner. A foreigner may reside in Spain but his heart will reside in his home country. He may think like a Spaniard but he will never be a Spaniard. Why? Because the history and culture of the country gives rise to different social customs and attitudes.

Some foreigners settle down and remain in Spain. Others go back home, their dream of a new life in the sun a failure. It is therefore important to understand the Spanish mentality and to adopt their way of life. Don't dash about, learn to relax, live for today and not tomorrow.

This book is a balance. It is not for the tourist. A legal expert would wish for more detail. An agent would not like the exposure of his commercial terms. It is, however, a step by step guide to buying a property in Spain, introducing the reader to the country, where to buy a property, the maze of documentation, the legal process and how to enjoy life to the full. The book, which is written in the financial language of the Euro, complements but is not a substitute for good legal advice which should always be sought and taken.

It also occupies a unique position in the market place. The managing director of a multi-national property company told me that 'The decision to purchase a Spanish property represents a defining moment in the lives of those so motivated and a book would be a most welcome addition to the genre'.

Harry King
Pedreguer, Spain

Acknowledgements

I wish to thank three people for helping me prepare this manuscript. Inmaculada Marquez Blazquez at the Instituto Konigin-Con Delfin was very anxious to correct my understanding of Spanish affairs. We did not agree on everything as we saw things from a different perspective. We did agree, however, that Spain was a young country, only three decades old, and changing fast.

My partner, Joan Stock, who has lived and worked in Spain for 12 years and has been exposed to the problems of trying to settle people in a country with a different culture. She spent hours translating the Appendixes of this book from obtuse Spanish legal wording into common sense English. She says that I speak Spanish with a Scottish accent but we both know it is the English language that is my problem!

This manuscript was originally conceived as an anecdotal look at life in Spain. Nikki Read talked me out of this. She was correct, for other, better written, more humorous books have since been published. What we now have is a book, not for the tourist or the lawyer, but for those blessed with common sense, who are considering buying a house in Spain. It is accurate information for the purchaser, hopefully a best seller for the publisher, and a source of pride for the author.

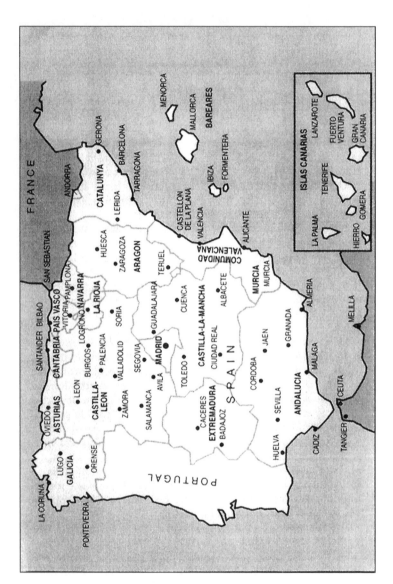

Fig. 1. A map of Spain.

1

Introducing Spain

A DREAM THAT CAN COME TRUE

Sitting on the porch, in the evening, holding a glass of wine, watching the sun setting over the sea, soon to be followed by a visit to the local *tapas* bar for some food and drinks. A holiday home or a retirement home in the sun is a dream, but one that can come true.

Whether your dream is a country house enveloped in vines, a secret retreat for golfing holidays, or a cosy apartment for the family to enjoy and drink too much Sangria, all you need is the courage of your own convictions. Whatever the goal, question not the sunny days ahead, merely your ambition to succeed.

Will it be a good investment?

For most middle-income people buying a Spanish property is not only affordable but also cheap. A well-appointed two-bedroom apartment on the Costa Blanca starts at only 80,000 Euros. Will the value of the property appreciate? As we start the new millennium the omens are good. Monetary control in Europe is tight. Interest rates are low. Inflation is down.

But care is required. In Spain the price of homes more than doubled between 1984 and 1990 largely because the supply of property could not keep pace with demand. From 1990 to 1997 price increases broadly matched inflation, but since then they have dramatically increased yet again. They are linked to the economies of other European countries, such as the United Kingdom and Germany, where in times of recession a property abroad may be one of the first things to be sacrificed. Equally a buoyant economy causes excess demand with a 12-month waiting time for new properties.

Spanish house prices may be low, but they are also volatile, appearing to appreciate in four to six year cycles.

Who buys a Spanish home?

A wide range of people buy a holiday home, particularly if it is near an airport, faces the sea or a golf course and the area has plenty of facilities. However, if it is a permanent retirement home then the average profile is of a couple, mid 50s and upwards, whose children have flown the nest. At least one partner will be an extrovert capable of dealing with the upheaval and change, so together they can look forward to their golden years with some enthusiasm.

It is not only northern Europeans who buy homes on the coast. Spain's growing wealth and fast growing economy has started to be reflected in Spaniards themselves buying holiday homes, although 'Madrid-on-Sea' tends to feature large family sized apartments, in shared complexes, with predominantly noisy Spanish neighbours.

Most people buy their Spanish home outright. If capital is required, a loan from a bank or a re-mortgage on the main residence are popular choices. Spanish banks offer mortgages at attractive rates. The golden rule is – if you earn in sterling, borrow in sterling and repay in sterling – but the Euro now gives greater flexibility to these traditional guidelines.

COMMON PERCEPTIONS

The Spanish dream is normally based on a number of perceptions. Most people have a preconceived idea of Spain. These perceptions are based on personal knowledge and experience. Telling people will not change their perception of a situation. It can only be altered by giving 'facts' in a learning situation.

Here are a few common perceptions about Spain.

Holidays

This first thought was probably gained during holidays on the Costas or on the Islands of Spain. It is a very positive perception with lots of sun, excellent wine and food, new friends, mixed up with a different culture. The formula is so good that repeat prescriptions are required and taken.

Life at home

The second perception, probably slightly negative, is of life and work at home. Long dark cold winters, only seeing daylight at the weekends. Rain, rain and more rain. When will it stop? Work seems to be getting more and more stressful. Computers, e-mail, faxes and the internet seem to have added to meetings, the telephone and the office memo. Company politics seem to have reached new levels. Playing politics used to be for advancement, now it's for survival. There is a feeling of being in a rut with a change necessary.

Practical thoughts

Of course the desire for change is coupled with a sense of pragmatism. One cannot just uproot oneself, avoid responsibility and dash off to sunny Spain. What about the finances? What about the willpower to succeed? What about parents and children; how will they feel? These issues need to be addressed before any move can be considered.

A big issue

The last perception is a complex summary of the previous three. One that says that the purchase of a property in Spain, either as a holiday home or a permanent residence, is a big, big issue, one

17

that needs many questions answered before coming to a
conclusion. But, providing the motivation is there, this quest for
knowledge will continue by reading books, looking at adverts in
newspapers, going to property exhibitions, visiting Spain and
talking to friends. The result will be an overall picture,
enabling a true perception of the country to be obtained.

LOOKING AT THE PROS AND CONS OF LIVING IN SPAIN

Spain isn't all sun, sea and sand. Living in Spain for long
periods is very different to a fortnight's package holiday. The
country may be the same, but the exposure to its people,
customs, culture and attitudes is radically different. As with all
countries there are a few downsides which aren't mentioned in
the holiday brochures and are only apparent when you live
there. Nothing alarming, you understand, but forewarned is
forearmed.

Climate

Hardly surprisingly the overwhelming attraction of Spain is its
excellent climate. It has a large landmass, with extensive high
plateaus and mountain ranges. The influence of the
Mediterranean and Atlantic produces a wide range of climatic
conditions. Summers everywhere are hot. In winter the north is
the wettest, the Costas and the Islands mild and surprisingly the
interior can drop below freezing.

Some parts of the Costa Blanca have been described by the
World Health Organisation as having one of the healthiest
climates in the world, a fact not overlooked when promoting
features of the area.

Climate has to be a balance. Not too hot, not too cold, a little
bit of rain to grow the crops, but not too much to deter people.
Some snow in the mountains for recreational purposes but not
enough to affect communications. Northern Spain has its lush

green pastures. The Costas offer sun and sand coupled with the clear blue waters of the Mediterranean. The southern rolling hills of Andalusia attract little movement in the blistering summer heat. The Balearic and Canary Islands are always pleasant. Madrid, the capital, is either freezing or roasting. Cordoba in the south is noted as the 'frying pan' of Europe.

The Mediterranean region has the best climatic balance:

- 320 days of sunshine per year

- 11.5 hours of sunshine per day in summer

- 14 inches of rain per year

- Average spring temperature 7 to 27 degrees centigrade

- Average summer temperature 17 to 36 degrees centigrade

- Average autumn temperature 9 to 30 degrees centigrade

- Average winter temperature 1 to 23 degrees centigrade.

While northern Europe is being deluged with rain, battered by wind, its roads closed by snow and ice, you can almost guarantee that Alicante and Malaga will be bathed in sunshine. But not all of Spain enjoys a Mediterranean climate. Here are some less attractive variations:

- San Sebastian – 41 inches of rain per year

- Madrid – average lowest winter temperature – minus 5 degrees centigrade

- Extremadura – average highest summer temperature – 41 degrees centigrade.

While there may be other reasons for coming to Spain, climate is the big, big number one. It is healthy, makes one feel good and, equally important, keeps the heating bills and domestic costs low.

Cost of living

Spain is no longer the cheap and cheerful country it once was. The cost of living has increased considerably over the last decade. However, with the exception of the large cities, the cost of living is still lower in coastal and rural areas than it is in the United Kingdom, Ireland, Germany and France. It is significantly lower than the cost of living in the Scandinavian countries and is on a par with Florida.

Of course a dominant factor in such a comparison is the relationship between the pound sterling and the Euro. British ex-pats who were paid in sterling during the first few millennium years received unprecedented exchange rates, but these are unlikely to be repeated as European monetary integration takes place.

The Spanish economy too affects the cost of living. Domestic running costs are less. Low central heating costs and low energy demand contribute to this. There is an abundance of locally produced food and wine, not only fresh from the market garden of Europe, but also cheap and plentiful. The beneficial effect of sunshine on day-to-day living costs is truly amazing. Sure, utility bill unit charges for water, electric, gas and telephone may be slightly high, but they are under government scrutiny and reducing annually. Thus overall, the total cost of living package is very much cheaper than its northern European equivalent.

Something for everyone

There is more to life in Spain than the Costas. Only a few miles inland, traditional unspoilt Spain opens up. The transformation is remarkable as high rise modern buildings, set in equally clean cities, are quickly left behind to be replaced by small white-walled villages and then, even further inland, by individual white houses scattered over hillsides. This is best typified on the Costa del Sol where, a few miles from the major city of Malaga, the white village of Competa is completely surrounded by thousands of individual white properties nestling on hillsides or sheltering in valleys.

There is a clever tourist poster of Andalusia which emphasises the diversity that Spain offers. It starts at the top with blue sky and sun, slightly lower down it has skiers on the snow capped Sierra Nevada, in the middle drawings of Moorish Granada, Sevilla, and Cordoba, near the bottom flamenco and bullfighting, and at the bottom the tourist resorts of Marbella, Malaga and Torremolinos facing a beach and Mediterranean sea. There really is something for everyone in Spain.

Some cities, which in the past have received negative publicity, are now recognising that their prime source of income is from tourism and have embarked on programmes to attract family groups. Benidorm, once home of the package holiday, now has manicured beaches, internationally recognised entertainment, top class restaurants, several theme parks and, on the outskirts, residential areas. Again, something for everyone.

The people

Anyone who has spent even a short time in Spain will know that its people are friendly. If you are polite, smile, and offer locals a greeting in their own language it will go a long way to establishing and maintaining relationships.

However, it would be fair to say in tourist resorts a perceived need to extract the maximum Euros in the minimum time has eroded some of the natural charm of the Spaniard. Some estate agents can be greedy. A few Spaniards too find it difficult to handle their new found wealth. But it would be wrong to characterise the whole country for the behaviour of a few.

Polite, welcoming and eager to please would be an accurate description of the average Señor and Señora. Perhaps a little bit slow, slightly shy, inward, and a little frustrating at times. Definitely bureaucratic in business, and sometimes unaware of a need for customer service. But unquestionably charming at all times.

As one might expect, there is a contrast between the older and younger generations. The more elderly Spaniard will have endured the repression of the Franco years, may be illiterate and have worked in agriculture. In contrast his offspring will be vibrant, computer literate, with a city based mentality that embraces new cosmopolitan values.

Medical facilities

Medical and dental facilities are among the best in Europe. There are many new hospitals staffed by highly qualified doctors and nurses. A high percentage of the cost of this service is provided from private resources. In addition to the local doctor's surgery, the chemist occupies a unique position in the medical hierarchy by providing remedies for simple ailments.

Crime

Spain does have a high petty crime rate. Homes have to be protected by security grilles on doors and windows. Cash, passports and electrical goods are the main targets. The theft of motor scooters is so high that insurance companies do not accept this risk. The police seem unable to reduce these incidents, so homeowners need to ensure protection of their own person and property.

Pickpockets, operating in gangs, are active at all open-air markets, indoor markets and within some supermarkets, particularly when thronged with people during the busy summer season.

It is wrong to point the finger at any nationality, social or occupational group because this is the result of increased prosperity within a tolerant society. While murder, bank robbery and crimes of passion are reported in the popular press these are a rarity. As long as sensible precautions are taken, the streets of Spain are safe for both adults and children.

Red tape

Unfortunately Spain is a nation of bureaucrats. Red tape stifles simple daily transactions and frustrates all nationalities including Spaniards themselves. It is very difficult to deal with, and most people opt out of the cycle by employing their own personal 'red-tape-cutter' known as a *gestor*.

Mañana

The last major downside of Spain is its cultural feature called *mañana* – never do something today if it can be put off to tomorrow, or the day after, or perhaps never to be done at all. To live successfully in Spain it is necessary to come to terms with its culture. Coping with *mañana* is a necessary skill that just has to be acquired. It is best seen with builders, repairmen, or when a car breaks down or indeed any occurrence requiring a commitment to a time or date. A shrug of the shoulders, an upturned hand, a slight bow of the head, a moment of silence is *mañana* in progress. Do not fight it, as no single person can change the culture of a nation. No matter how difficult, learn to live with it.

A PICTURE OF THE COUNTRY

History

The Iberian Peninsula, like most Mediterranean countries, has been invaded many times. The Phoenicians, the Greeks, the

Carthaginians, the Celts, the Romans and the Visigoths, six different invaders, take us only to the year 711. Then the good guys arrive. They were the Arab and Berber invaders, now popularly known as the Moors, who called Spain 'Al Andalus'.

Dominant in the south of the country, the Moors established a rich heritage around Cordoba where mathematics, science, architecture and decorative arts flourished. Some of the finest architectural masterpieces can be found today in the Andalusian cities of Granada, Jaen, Sevilla and Cordoba. The Alhambra at Granada is universally recognised as being the jewel in a rich crown, one place in the world where Jews, Christians and Arabs lived peacefully together. Their impact extended into the development of farming through the establishment of terraces with irrigation systems and, unseen, the development of a competent political administration system.

Nothing stands still. A re-conquest followed with the foundation of a Spanish state. This led to the voyages of Columbus to the New World. From 1492 Spaniards attempted to extend their rule worldwide by conquering Mexico, Peru and Chile, destroying in the process Indian civilisations, and returning home with great wealth in the form of gold and silver.

This did not last. The next three hundred years saw a succession of wars, the loss of its Empire, increasing instability in government with a consequent slow decline in economic wealth and influence.

An increasingly weary nation saw nationalist generals, led by Franco, rise against the government in 1936 and the start of the Spanish Civil War (see Figure 2). Supported by Hitler and Mussolini, Spain was an international outcast. Although a dictatorship was established, with an often brutal rule, all was not bad as a slow, painful reconstruction of the country began. The economy strengthened and started to boom in the 1960s as northern Europe's wealth enabled its peoples to visit the sunshine of Spain for the first time. The influx of different cultures and international pressures brought social liberalisation

1996	Election of a coalition led by Aznar
1996	Spain joins the EU. It benefits from subsidies
1981	Military officers unsuccessfully attempt a *coup d'etat* to overthrow democracy
1975	Death of Franco. Juan Carlos proclaimed King. Modern Spain is born
1962	Tourism on the Mediterranean given the official go ahead
1959	Founding of ETA, the Basque separatist group
1953	USA bases on Spanish soil in exchange for economic aid
1945	At the end of the Second World War, Spain is diplomatically and politically isolated
1939	Franco declares the end of the Civil War
1937	Nationalists declare Franco Head of State. Six months later Nazi planes bomb northern Spanish towns

Fig. 2. Recent history.

long before Franco's death and the arrival of democracy in 1978.

A new country

Modern Spain is a monarchy under King Juan Carlos. It is a tolerant society with many different customs and lifestyles. Since 1985 Spain has been a full member of the EU taking both European and international politics seriously.

It is a tightly regulated country having five levels of government. The top two levels comprise a congress and senate of elected representatives from the provinces, the islands and the regions. There are 17 autonomous regions, called *Comunidades*, with their own parliaments and governments. This has led to a massive duplication of bureaucracy, because in addition to its own parliament each *comunidade* also has separate representation from the state. The autonomous regions are further divided into provinces and then into the smaller *municipio*.

Following the death of Franco and the country's release from
his oppressive dictatorship, Spain has transformed itself into a
tolerant, democratic society but one still trying to shake off the
shackles of the era when heavyweight bureaucracy ruled the
day. Although great strides have been made there is still a long
way to go as the decentralised government, a function of
establishing a democracy, battles with duplication of effort and
unnecessary bureaucracy evidenced in the property
conveyancing process and in the procedures involved in taking
up permanent residency in Spain.

Jose Maria Aznar, a centre right politician, has been Prime
Minister of Spain since 1996. He has concentrated on improving
Spain's public finances. The country has benefited greatly from
the EU programme of special economic aid to poorer countries.
Internally it is still troubled by the Basque separatist group
called ETA. In 1999 border controls were tightened to Gibraltar
in order to pressurise the British government over its stance on
sovereignty.

Today's Spain

The country as we know it now has been established for only 30
years. The economy has boomed. Traditional agriculture has
declined. The importance of manufacturing and tourism has
increased. A new motorway network has opened up the country.
Building is taking place everywhere. The pace of change is
dramatic, purposeful and peaceful. Its people, so long
oppressed, are now vibrant, confident, open, tolerant and
justifiably proud of their achievements. With the Olympic
Games, European Games and Expo Exhibitions being held in
Spain in the last few years the world is seeing Spain competing
and winning at an international level.

DEMOGRAPHICS

Mainland Spain covers an area of half a million square kilometres and has a coastline of 2,100 kilometres. Spain includes both the Canary and Balearic Islands. It is the second largest country in Europe after France. The interior of Spain is a vast plateau called the Meseta bound to the north east by the Pyrenees, in the south west by the Sierra Morena and in the south by the best known Sierra Nevada. Across the Meseta itself many rivers have cut deep valleys. Much of the coastline is steep and rocky but there is a narrow coastal plain bordering the Mediterranean.

Population

The population of 40 million is less than many European countries. Spain, despite being predominantly a Catholic country, has a low birth rate and a high life expectancy of 75 years for men and 80 for women. Many Spaniards are now urban dwellers, Madrid the capital being the largest conurbation. Half a million British live in Spain, concentrated in the capital, Barcelona, the Costas and the Islands.

Language

Castilian Spanish is the romance language of the country. Catalan, modified French, is spoken in the north east. Valenciano is another, difficult to understand, regional dialect. Two hundred million people speak Spanish world wide, mainly in the former Spanish Empire, making it the third most popular language after English and Chinese. English is a business language in Madrid and Barcelona. It is well understood in the Costas and Islands, but is rarely spoken or understood in rural areas.

Main cities

The principal cities are Madrid, situated in the geographical
centre of mainland Spain, the seat of central government and an
important commercial centre, followed by Barcelona, a
commercial and industrial city with a large port. There is an
intense rivalry between the two cities, both political and
sporting. Bilbao on the northern coast is a modern port.
Valencia, facing the Mediterranean, is an important area for car
manufacturing. Sevilla in the south west exports agricultural
produce such as olive oil, fruit and wine.

Economy

Spain has changed from a tradition of agriculture to that of a
semi industrial nation, although it still has the largest fishing
fleet in Europe. Ten per cent of the workforce are now engaged
in tourism with only 10% in agriculture and 1% in fishing.
Encouraged by EU grants, industry is expanding rapidly. The
construction of new colourful buildings is clearly visible
alongside main roads. There is a huge, duplicated civil service.

Although high by some European standards, the current level
of unemployment at 8.5% is the lowest since 1979. The
unemployment rate for women is two and a half times the rate
for men. The recent reduction in unemployment is attributed to
an expansion in the construction and service industries.

The people

Social customs have changed. People are much less formal.
Familiarity is a hallmark of Spanish life. Handshaking and
kissing on the cheek is the usual form of greeting. Old fashioned
courtliness and formal manners are, however, still the custom in
rural areas. Great store is set by personal loyalty and friendship,
but it is also very important to take account of a Spaniard's
personal sense of honour and pride, which is easily offended.

The extended family is the main social unit with family ties being very strong.

SUMMARY

- Acquiring a Spanish property in the sun is a dream, but one that can come true.

- Although we all have perceptions of Spain they need to be corrected, enhanced or confirmed.

- Spain has a glorious climate, a reasonably low cost of living, a tolerant society and contains something for everyone.

- Its people are charming.

- It suffers from a high petty crime rate, governmental bureaucracy and an irritating social habit called *mañana*.

- Spain is a modern, vibrant country having shaken off its less than glorious past and now focusing its economy on industry and tourism.

2

Narrowing the Options

PLANNING TO GO

Festivals, cultural events and sports competitions crowd the
Spanish calendar. Even small villages have at least one
traditional fiesta, lasting a week or more, when parades,
bullfights and fireworks replace work. Many rural and coastal
towns celebrate the harvest or fishing catch with a gastronomic
fair where local produce can be sampled. Music, dance, drama
and festivals are held in the major cities throughout the year.
The country's favourite outdoor sports culminate in several
national championships. The property seeker, however, has to
put these events to one side. Attractive they may well be, but a
more focused approach is required, as the seasons magnify or
hide some of Spain's more interesting characteristics.

Spring

Life in Spain moves outdoors with the arrival of Spring. Cafes
fill with people. The countryside is at its best as wild flowers
bloom before the onset of the summer heat. Water flows to
crops, giving a green look to a sometimes barren landscape. This
is a good time to look at property. Everything is fresh and clean.
The summer crowds are absent.

Summer

August is Spain's big holiday season. Big cities empty as
Spaniards flock to the coast or to the mountains to escape the
searing heat of the interior. Their numbers are swelled by

millions of foreign tourists. Entertainment and eating only take place in the cool of the evening, when temperatures drop. In the late summer fiestas are everywhere. But it is hot, it is stifling and there are too many people. Some do go to look at property, but it is an exhausting business.

Autumn

After the heat of summer, before the rainy season, the countryside, roads and property have a dirty, unwashed, and unattractive appearance as a thin film of dust covers the landscape.

Towards the end of this quarter the rain arrives, sometimes heavy torrential rain. The northern tourist resorts practically close down. But the harvesting of crops continues, with grape and wine production taking over as the main cultural and agricultural activity. The hunting season begins.

Winter

It is always said that winter is a good time to view property. The other side of the coin is seen as urbanisations empty, many restaurants close, and coastal resorts appear quite desolate. Winter does vary greatly from region to region. In the high mountains, snowfalls bring skiers to the slopes, while in the lower areas, olives, oranges and lemons are being gathered. The cold of Madrid contrasts with the warmth of the Canaries' high tourist season. Christmas is a special time for family reunions, giving presents, sharing food and attending religious celebrations. The first rays of spring are eagerly awaited.

DECIDING WHERE TO GO

Northern Europeans, when considering Spain, tend to favour living near, or just a few kilometres from, the sea. Consequently,

Statistic	Spain	Ireland	Germany	UK
% labour force in agriculture	10	13.5	9	12
% labour force in industry	33	29	38	29
% labour force in services	55	57	58	69
births per 1000 people	10	13.5	9	12
people per sq. kilometre	75	50	230	240
cars per 1000 people	380	270	500	370

Fig. 3. Statistics.
Source: Encarta

in order to describe the country, we will divide Spain into
coastal areas.

- Northern Spain, running from west to east, and facing the
  Atlantic Ocean, comprises the six *comunidades* of Galicia,
  Asturias, Cantabria, the Basque Country, Navarra and La
  Rioja.

- Eastern Spain comprises Aragon which faces the Pyrenees,
  and running from north to south Catalonia, Valencia and
  Murcia, all of which face the eastern Mediterranean embrace
  well known places such as the Costa Brava, the Costa
  Dorada, the Costa Azahar and the universally acknowledged
  Costa Blanca.

- Southern Spain comprises of only one *comunidade*, the
  largest and best known, Andalucia, which faces in two
  directions: the Costa del Sol bordering the Mediterranean and
  the Costa de la Luz facing the Atlantic Ocean.

- In the heart of the country central Spain comprises the four
  comunidades of Madrid, Castilla-la Mancha, Extremadura,
  and Castilla y Leon.

- Spain's islands comprise of the popular Balearics in the east Mediterranean and the Canaries set to the south-west in the warm waters of the Atlantic.

GREEN NORTHERN SPAIN

Increasing numbers of people are discovering the deep green landscapes, the solitude of the mountains and the quiet sandy beaches of northern Spain. The Atlantic coast from the Portuguese border to the Pyrenees is often scenic but no more so than the cliffs of Galicia and the Picos mountains. Inland the mild but wet climate has created lush green meadows and broad-leaved forests. A famous medieval pilgrimage route to the city of Santiago de Compostela crosses the region.

Food

Some of the most delicious seafood comes from the Atlantic coast with specialities including mussels, scallops, lobsters and octopus. The north coast also supplies crabs, fat anchovies and tuna. Soft and blue cheese comes from the Cantabrian mountains. But it is wine that gives this region its fame. Spain's most prestigious red wine, Rioja, is matured to a distinctive vanilla mellowness as the grape is influenced during its growth on the hilly stony soil by both the Mediterranean and Atlantic weather systems.

Places of interest

Galicia, to the west, has as its centrepiece the beautiful old city of Santiago de Compostela. Surrounded by forest covered hills, the way of life seems to have changed little in centuries.

To the east in Asturias and Cantabria, the most obvious attraction is the group of mountains called the Picos de Europa which straddles the two communities. These mountains, set in a national park, offer excellent rock climbing and good hiking, but in winter, when covered in snow, are extremely dangerous.

Further east lies the Basque Country, Navarra and La Rioja, a green hilly region, offering the diverse sporting attractions of the Pyrenees. It includes the fine city of San Sebastian, gloriously situated on a neat shell shaped bay and now recognised as an elegant and fashionable resort renowned for its great summer arts festivals – jazz, classical music and film. It is also home to the Basques, a group suppressed under Franco's regime, but since the arrival of democracy they have their own parliament and their own police force. Although always wishing for more, they have great autonomy over their own affairs.

Looking to buy a property in northern Spain? Many do. Some people say it is like Scotland, Ireland, Wales and England rolled into one. Mild, wet and definitely green. Just like being at home but with a different culture. The Swiss too lay claim to the country, saying the Picos are similar to their Alps.

As with all of Spain, the benefits of this region are to be found outdoors, in the countryside, in the mountains, by the sea, living in towns and villages, sampling the different foods and lifestyle.

DIVERSE EASTERN SPAIN

This is a large area encompassing Aragon, Catalonia, Valencia and Murcia popularly referred to as Barcelona, the eastern Pyrenees, and the Costas – Brava, Dorada, Azahar and Blanca.

Food

Although Catalonia may be famous for its controversial painter Salvador Dali, today it is more importantly known for good food. *Amanida* is a salad with vegetables, cured meat, cheese and fish. *Sequet* is a fish and shellfish stew. Sausages come in all shapes, sizes and colours. The most famous is a pudding called *Crema Catalan*: a rich egg custard with a golden brown layer of grilled sugar on top, served very cold.

Valencia has its famous *paella*, a dish known world wide. It is cooked traditionally in a large, shallow, two handled pan over an open fire. Short grained rice, grown on the nearby plain, is cooked with a mixture of ingredients, notably seafood, chicken, rabbit, pork, tomatoes, peppers, saffron and of course garlic.

Barcelona

Anyone looking for premier city living? This, unquestionably, is the place. One of the Mediterranean's busiest ports, it is much more than the capital of Catalonia. Culturally, commercially and in sport it not only rivals Madrid, but rightfully considers itself on a par with the greatest European cities. The success of the Olympic Games confirmed this to the world. It is always open to outside influences because of its location on the coast, not too far from the French border.

Las Ramblas is the most famous street in Spain. It is busy round the clock, especially in the evenings and at weekends. News stands, caged birds, flower stalls, tarot readers, musicians and mime artists throng the wide, tree shaded, central walkway.

Camp Nou is one of Europe's largest football stadiums, home to the city's famous football club with its fanatical, critical supporters. Its magnificent sweeping structure befits one of the world's richest clubs. Barcelona FC more than anything else is a symbol of Catalan nationalism pitted against the central government of Madrid. To fail to win the league is one thing, to come behind Real Madrid is a complete disaster.

Barcelona is a city with impeccable style and vitality, demonstrated by the very best of Catalan, Spanish and international fashion design. It is complemented by a stunning live arts scene as it regularly plays host to some of the world's best musicians.

The downside . . . life in an apartment block and they don't come any bigger than the huge skyscrapers of Barcelona.

Aragon and Catalonia

On their northern borders these *comunidades* butt onto the
Pyrenees and France. Catalonia additionally faces east to the
Mediterranean, giving us the first taste of two Costas – Brava
and Dorada.

Aragon stretches almost half the length of Spain and is
bisected by the Ebro, one of the country's longest rivers. It takes
in a wide variety of scenery, from the snow-capped mountains
of the Ordesa National Park in the Pyrenees to the dry plains of
the interior. The major cities are Teruel and the capital Zaragoza,
Spain's fifth largest city. The climate of the region varies as
much as the landscape with the winters long and harsh and the
summers very hot. Northern Europeans generally don't settle in
Aragon unless they are in love with the Pyrenees. Property is
very scarce. Even barns for conversion are impossible to obtain.

Catalonia presents an altogether different picture. A proud
nation within a nation, with its own language, Catalan, which
has all but replaced Spanish in place names and on road signs
throughout the region. The language, now fully recovered from
the ban it suffered under Franco's dictatorship, is spoken by
eight million people and is akin to the Provencal of France. Its
major cities are Taragona and of course Barcelona, the region's
capital, economically and culturally important enough to rival
Madrid.

In the 1960s the rugged Costa Brava (wild coast) became one
of Europe's first mass package holiday destinations. Tourism
quickly followed to the long sandy stretches of the Costa
Dorada (golden coast).

Communications are good, the motorway from France
traverses Eastern Spain on its long way south to Gibraltar. The
area is also well served by train and bus services.

Where to live? Well, we have already mentioned the fine city
of Barcelona. It is perhaps better to miss the mass tourist resorts
of Loret del Mar, Tossa del Mar, La Platja d'Aro, Stiges and
Salou. But on the coast some smaller towns deserve a visit. Try

Cadaques, Sant Feliu de Guixols, Palamos and Blanes. Inland Girona, a handsome town set on the River Onyar, is well worth considering.

Valencia and Murcia

More popularly known as the Costa del Azahar (orange blossom) and the Costa Blanca (white coast) this area is distinguished by its fine climate. The principal holiday resorts are Benidorm, Torrevieja and Mar Menor. It has fine commercial centres at Valencia, Spain's third largest city; Alicante, the main city on the Costa Blanca; Cartagena, a former naval base, and of course Murcia, a lively university city. Tucked away to the south is an almost unknown area called the Costa Calida. It is thinly populated and well off the beaten track.

Close to the sea there are several scenic nature reserves – the freshwater lagoons of L'Albufera, the salt pans of Torrevieja and the limestone crag of the Penya d'Ifach. Inland the mountains around Alcoi await discovery, and the green Jalon Valley remains undeveloped.

Having warmer winters than the Costa Brava, cheaper and less fashionable than the Costa del Sol, the Costa Blanca occupies a prime stretch of Mediterranean coastline with Alicante's airport and main line railway station a major communication hub. Long sandy beaches, in places lined with hotels and apartment blocks, are a feature of the area. North of Altea cliffs, coves, hills and greenery break the scenery but to the south around Torrevieja it is barren, dry and flat.

Torrevieja

Anyone looking for property will invariably come across the town of Torrevieja, the fastest expanding town in Europe where, since the mid 80s houses have been built at a prodigious rate. In the next five years new homes are planned to be built at the rate of 6,000 units per year. Selling these homes either for permanent residence, holiday, or to let, is a major marketing exercise with companies all over Europe competing with a portfolio of detached, semi detached, terraced and apartment style properties. European property exhibitions will always feature Torrevieja. What is the attraction? Properties here are cheap, the climate excellent, and communications are good. The downside – in summer it is wall to wall with people. The beaches are packed, and the restaurants are full. In winter, the white urbanisations are mostly uninhabited.

Places of interest

Prestigious property areas are the picturesque towns and surrounding areas of Denia, Javea, Moraira, Calpe and Altea being much favoured by the British, German, Dutch and Swiss. To the south is a playground for the rich at La Manga, where pampered sporting activities and expensive homes in exclusive surroundings are the order of the day.

ANDALUCIA – SOUTHERN SPAIN

So to Andalucia, a large area extending across the south of the country incorporating the deserts of Almeria, the wetlands of Donana, the snow-capped peaks of the Sierra Nevada and the beaches of the Costa del Sol. The inland cities of Granada, Cordoba and Sevilla share a rich Moorish heritage. It is the home of many white walled villages. The capital Sevilla rivals Barcelona for fine city living.

Food

The food of this area has been heavily influenced by its historic Arab inhabitants. Traditionally almonds, rice, lemons, oranges, grapes and olives were grown. Today's crops now include strawberries, apples, melons, cherries and pears. Gazpacho, a soup served chilled, is made from olive oil, garlic, tomatoes, cucumber, vinegar and peppers. Barbecued meats, sauces flavoured with cumin or saffron, sweets made from crushed almonds are all typical dishes. Grilled fish, especially sardines and *calamares* (squid), and whole fish baked in a crust of salt, are popular dishes.

Sevilla

El Arenal, a district of Sevilla, was once home to an ammunition factory and artillery headquarters but now the atmosphere is set by the city's majestic bullring called the Plaza de Toros de la Maestranza. During the bull-fighting season the bars and restaurants are packed, but for the rest of the year the wide Quadalquivir River is enjoyed by many on boat trips. The *barrio* of Santa Cruz is Sevilla's other district. It was the old Jewish quarter: a warren of white alleyways and flower decked patios, now representing Sevilla at its most romantic and compact. The maze of narrow streets hide tapas bars, plazas, and up-market residences. Ornamental orange trees line the streets, their bittersweet taste suitable for making marmalade. It was, however, Expo '92 which focused world attention on Sevilla where over one hundred countries were represented in the many pavilions which displayed scientific, technological and cultural exhibits.

Although hot, Sevilla has excellent shopping facilities with some European chain stores represented in its modern streets. Premier living is available in this city where all the stereotypes of Andalusia meet in its capital. Town houses are available. There are few big apartment blocks. By travelling only a few kilometres from the city walls the rural delights of the countryside open up and detached white walled properties are available at very reasonable prices.

Almeria

To the west lies Almeria. This major crop growing area is covered by acres and acres of plastic sheeting as it is a huge supplier of fruit and vegetables to the rest of Europe. A pleasant place is Mojacar, its white houses cascading over a lofty ridge inland from a long sandy beach. People settle here. The area is noted for Europe's only desert, the Trabernas, made famous as the location for spaghetti Westerns such as 'The Good, the Bad and the Ugly' starring Clint Eastwood.

Costa del Sol

It may be one the most over developed strips of coastline in the world, but thanks to 300 days of sunshine per year this area of Spain is home to many. It hosts the jet set sophistication of Marbella, and over 30 golf courses lying just inland. There are many resorts aimed at the mass tourist market, but some of the older developments, just south of Malaga, have a tired, well-worn look, with planners now facing the difficult task of possible demolition.

The highlight of the area is unquestionably Marbella, a stylish resort with Puerto Banus its ostentatious marina. Expensive shops, restaurants and glittering nightlife reflect the wealth of its inhabitants and visitors. Close behind is the up and coming Sotogrande, an exclusive resort of luxury villas with a marina and golf course. Estepona is quieter, not so built-up and not attached to the long concrete strip that unfortunately is a characteristic of this Costa. Nerja and Almunecar too are gleaming white modern towns, good examples of popular residential areas. Malaga is another fine city with a thriving port. Its new shopping centre presents an interesting blend of the old and the new.

There are other towns but for the property seeker it is best to give them a miss. A home of high rise holiday hotels, perhaps less brash than it was, adequately describes Torremolinos and Fuengirola.

A few miles inland from the coast at Malaga a different Spain opens up. Lots of greenery, with many thousands of classical white houses covering the slopes of rounded hills. Even small towns are cut into the contours of the landscape. For a person looking for something different, and wishing to blend into the lifestyle of Andalucia, then this is the place to be. Many people move here, their initial hard toil being rewarded with an individual property, either carefully renovated or newly designed. This is the land of the *finca*, a country house surrounded by orange, lemon, olive and almond trees, possibly lacking in all mod cons, but well away from other humans. It is rural life . . . where time is not important.

Gibraltar

Gibraltar is not in Spain. It is governed by the United Kingdom. Joint sovereignty seems to be the way ahead but in the meantime, economically it stands alone. It's future as a strategic entrance to the Mediterranean seems less important as time goes by. A small community, isolated from the rest of Spain by artificial political barriers, it's future is uncertain. The economy of the Rock depends on a naval dockyard, tourism, tax-free shopping and financial services. There are few houses to buy.

Costa de la Luz

The Coast of Light is situated to the west of Gibraltar facing the Atlantic. Spain's southernmost tip is an unspoilt, windswept stretch of coast characterised by strong pure light – hence the name. Other than Cadiz, which is almost entirely surrounded by water; Jerez, the capital of sherry production; the Donana National Park, an area of wetlands, sand dunes and marshland – the region has little to commend itself. Few people settle here.

41

Inland

Instead of settling on the fertile plains, some Andalusians chose to live in fortified hilltop towns now known as *pueblos blancos* (white towns) whitewashed in the Moorish tradition and today working agricultural villages. Ronda is the most well known. It is generally accepted that there are eight or nine white working towns, more suitable for touring or visiting than for residence. Similarly the Alpujarras, on the southern slopes of the Sierra Nevada, has many irregularly shaped white houses clinging to its hillsides.

Granada and Cordoba are old Moorish cities. Surprisingly, given the culture of the Alhambra, a Moorish piece of architecture representing paradise on earth and regarded as the eighth wonder of the world, Granada is a relatively inexpensive place to live. The benefits of hiking and skiing in the nearby Sierra Nevada mountains compensate a little for the cold winters and baking hot summers.

VAST CENTRAL SPAIN

The vast central plateau is covered in dry dusty plains and large rolling fields. Given the attractions of the Costas and the Islands it is not an area where many northern Europeans settle. It is a place of work. The region is dominated by long straight roads, vast fields devoted to wheat, sunflowers and the grape. It is remote, of stunning beauty, suitable for those engaged in agriculture or for those who want to get off the beaten track, going back to nature in old rural Spain.

The adventures of Don Quixote are celebrated. He is represented in metal figures everywhere.

Food

Game such as wild boar, pheasant and partridge is plentiful in Central Spain. La Mancha maintains a tradition of robust cooking with a variety of one-pot pulse stews. Castilla y Leon is known for its suckling pig and milk fed lamb roasted whole in enormous bread ovens. Many convents and shops in Toledo continue to make popular little marzipan cakes.

The region is well known for *cocido madrileno*, a beef stew, *patatas a la importancia*, which are egg-coated potatoes fried and then simmered in wine, and Spain's famous manchego cheese made from sheep's milk.

Madrid

Situated in the centre of the country is the capital Madrid, a city of over three million people and a hub for rail, road and air travel as befits a modern capital. Its altitude of 660 metres gives rise to a classic temperature profile of cold winters and hot summers, making spring and autumn the best times to visit. Those who can escape from Madrid during August make for the cooler north or south to the Mediterranean.

Despite the climate the capital city has developed its own unique personality. It boasts the Parque del Retiro, a world famous area of leafy paths and avenues, a royal palace and grand public squares. Its museums are filled with Spain's historic treasures. The Museo del Prado contains the world's greatest assembly of Spanish painting, particularly the works of Velazquez and Goya. It also houses impressive foreign collections.

Madrid is a city that offers the best in shopping facilities. The latest designer clothes are sold in elegant up-market stores. There are food markets throughout the city. The centuries-old Rastro, open every Sunday, is one of the world's greatest flea markets.

There is a good choice of music: classical, jazz and rock competing with Madrid's own comic style opera known as *zarzuela*. Saturday night starts in the cafes, moves to the tapas bars, restaurants or clubs, revelling throughout the night and adding to the city's clamouring traffic noise.

THE HOLIDAY ISLANDS

Spain's two groups of islands lie in separate seas. The Balearics are in the Mediterranean and the Canaries in the Atlantic, off the African coast. The islands, blessed with a warm climate, good beaches and clear waters, are visited by many thousands of people each year.

Food

Regional food is gradually being squeezed out, but traditional egg dishes can still be eaten in good Mallorcan restaurants.

In the Canary islands, however, regional food does not exist, forgotten in the commercial need to provide international blandness. Bananas are grown here, a small, sweet variety, often used in fritters and tarts.

The Balearics

Often associated with mass inexpensive tourism, these islands have something for everyone. For those turning their back on the bustle of coastal resorts with all their attractions, the countryside and old towns lie relatively undisturbed. The Balearics have white villages, wooded hills and caves. Mallorca, a culturally rich island, has mountains to go with the sea and shore. Ibiza is known for its nightlife. Menorca and Formentera are quieter, more tranquil.

Mallorca is a good choice for living. Access is usually by air, but there are also excellent ferry services from Barcelona, Valencia, Alicante or Denia. The west coast, from Andratx to Pollenca and the Gallic influence of Soller, is particularly attractive. Palma, the capital, is a clean, bustling city.

Property tends to be expensive as is the cost of living with everything imported except fruit and wine.

Canary Islands

Poised on the edge of the tropics west of Morocco, the Canaries enjoy plentiful sunshine, pleasantly cooled by the trade winds. The Canaries have extraordinary volcanic landscapes unlike any other part of Spain and contain no less than four national parks. The scenery ranges from lava desert to forest, from sand dunes to volcanic mountains. There are seven islands: Tenerife, Gran Canaria and Lanzarote are the largest.

Tenerife is dominated by Mount Teide, an awesome sight, the highest mountain in Spain. Volcanic material forms a wilderness of weathered, mineral tinted rocks. A single road runs through the area, passing a hotel, cable car station and a visitors' centre. Los Cristianios is an old fishing port, which has developed into a pleasant town along the foothills of a barren landscape.

The capital of Gran Canaria is called Las Palmas, yet another fine city. Playa del Ingles is a holiday area of high rise hotel and apartment blocks best avoided. Puerto Rico and Puerto del Mogan, on the other hand, are attractive, unique, pretty places, quite the opposite to the brash concrete holiday resorts.

Lanzarote is sparsely populated, with more goats than people. There is no water. No industry apart from tourism. Solitude, sun worshipping and water sports occupy a day where time has no meaning.

Housing can be readily found. So too can timeshares. These islands are home to many a persuaded person, now restricted by selling regulations.

SUMMARY

- The best time to look at Spanish property is in the spring, when the country is green and fresh.

- For new permanent residents a check during the winter months is desirable. Urbanisations are then deserted, hill sides sparsely populated and some facilities closed.

- Northern Europeans tend to settle in very specific areas.

- For city living, Barcelona closely followed by Sevilla are recommended. San Sebastian, Alicante, Malaga and Palma are other fine cities. Notwithstanding the temperature, Madrid has much to offer.

- Northern Spain, wet, mild and green, often reminds people of home.

- The Costa Blanca with its excellent climate is highly recommended but care has to be taken in fast expanding towns to ensure the dream house of today is not set in a concrete jungle of tomorrow.

- Some areas with potential remain in the overdeveloped Costa del Sol. Try Estepona. Inland to Andalucia opportunities abound for an individual renovated property.

- The islands have an excellent climate, mainly attracting people for holidays and more expensive for day to day living.

- That little bit extra can be found in Denia, Javea, Calpe and Altea. Something more exclusive at Marbella and Sotogrande. Mojacar, Nerja and Almunecar offer compact living in clean white towns. Soller is different. Puerto del Mogan is a bit special.

3

Making a Start

READING NEWSPAPERS

Looking at newspapers and gazing in the window of an estate agent is a quite normal method of starting the search for a new home. After all the newspapers have large property sections, sometimes greater than the news content itself. Similarly a walk down the main street of any town will see a number of estate agents displaying for sale many attractively photographed properties. This initial browsing may not take place with any specific intent, but merely to give a feel of style, price and location.

Finding a property in Spain follows a similar course, but on a much larger scale.

Each week in the popular daily press and the Sunday press there are dozens of adverts for Spanish properties. They often have a drawing or photograph tending to emphasise a low cost, high specification property in a sunny location.

Of course there are English language newspapers published in Spain. As you would expect they too have large property sections. Living elsewhere in Europe, it is sometimes difficult to get hold of these newspapers but contacting the publishers should result in one being sent by post (see Appendix 8). Here are the main titles:

- *The Costa Blanca News* – a well read publication.
- *The Costa del Sol News* – equally popular.
- *Sur in English* – the big one for the Costa del Sol.
- *The Entertainer* – a free paper based in the east of Spain.

- *The Mallorca Daily Bulletin.*
- *The Island Gazette* – for the Canary Islands.

GOING TO PROPERTY EXHIBITIONS

Moving from 'passive to active' mode means making a positive commitment. This commitment is the first real step to the fulfilment of a dream. Armchair contemplation is now over. Going to an exhibition is metaphorically getting one's feet wet. Property exhibitions are commonplace: small ones run in hotels throughout the year, large ones in conference or exhibition centres in the spring and summer. Some are specifically targeted at Spain but the larger exhibitions may also have representatives promoting properties in Florida and Cyprus.

Objectives

Before going to a property exhibition, you need crystal clear objectives. This is not the time to fall for the seductive charms of some salesperson. Nor is it the time to be woolly headed. What is the object of your visit? Here are a few suggestions.

- To confirm your perceptions about the area of your choice.
- To obtain more facts about properties, styles and prices.
- To acquire brochures, particularly those with property plans and photographs.
- To prepare a list of questions to be answered.
- To choose an agent, one who has sincerity, knowledge, and most importantly, the widest selection of properties to sell.
- Lastly, if relaxed about these facts, to plan a visit to Spain to look at some property.

The exhibition

It is a colourful, noisy affair. Orange and yellow are the dominant colours, not only representing the Spanish flag, but the

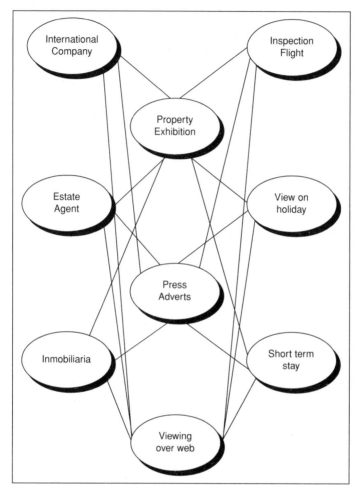

Fig. 4. The viewing choice.

lemon and orange crops. The noise is people talking, with much verbal fencing, displays of knowledge or lack of it, or holiday locations being revisited. Salespeople are anxious to 'close'. Visitors are still wary, asking questions, getting facts. Sangria, the mass Spanish anti-depressant, is usually available.

What of the exhibitor? They may be an international company, or an estate agent or a small Spanish business. What are their objectives? It is not to sell a house since they do not have the necessary detailed, up to the minute information to hand. It is simply to move people to the next step in the selling process by giving facts and persuading them to go on a ridiculously cheap inspection flight.

VIEWING ALTERNATIVES

The importance of choosing the best method of viewing a Spanish property cannot be overestimated. There are three options: inspection flights, viewing while on holiday or renting a property for a short period to look around. Let's look at the advantages and disadvantages of all three.

Inspection flights

A three day, escorted, highly focused visit to an area of your choice. The flights are cheap, a hotel is booked, and entertainment is laid on. Viewing is from the comfort of a mini-bus with only a short stroll to each show house. The ambience of the area is highlighted. From the properties shown most people can decide what is best for their own circumstances. It is, however, a pressurised trip, where time and space to think are at a premium. It does not give freedom to appreciate the bigger picture, or the true ambience of the town or countryside. It is a snapshot at a point in time.

Inspection flights depart almost every week, normally covering three or four nights over a weekend. These trips, by charter or scheduled flight, are solely for the potential purchasers of a property. Before travelling people are reminded of the currency and deposit arrangements required to secure a purchase.

Holidays

While giving more potential viewing time than an inspection flight, the use of this time is less focused. It is not possible to be escorted everywhere for a fortnight. When on a family holiday the emphasis is on enjoyment, on the area itself and on its facilities. Usually, it is only when this is satisfied that the more specific aspects of house hunting can begin.

Short term rental

Simply the best method. It gives all the necessary time to consider the options. It is no longer a snapshot in time. Property and location can be considered at leisure. But it can take a good few months, leaving this option open only to those retiring or with time available.

THE INTERNATIONAL COMPANY

Big international property companies have marketing and sales offices in all European countries. In Spain the selling package continues with prospective clients moving along a highly organised conveyor belt. Of course an inspection trip is geared to the needs of the individual! Of course the client does not have to buy! Or so they say. However, it is also fair to say the package offered by these companies is impressive. It covers inspection flights, property inspection, selling, bank and solicitor selection and most importantly assistance during the difficult moving-in stage.

These companies tend to dominate the marketplace in which they operate, namely new property sales. By focusing on one area they drive costs down. The huge scale of their operation gives the customer a wide choice. Their influence spreads to property design and development.

All large companies can attract criticism, particularly those in a service industry. The only valid criticism of international property companies is their lack of flexibility, which is directly related to the size of their operation. Big international companies are the trend-setters of the marketplace. Many try to follow with a smaller, more individualistic, more personalised offering.

ESTATE AGENTS

No one lays claim to the much-derided label 'estate agent'. Preference is given to names such as 'International Property Consultant', or perhaps 'Blue Sky Property' or even a more focused 'Torrecasa Property Company'. Whatever the title of the company, it is designed to reflect an image, removed as far as possible from that of an old fashioned estate agency.

And quite right too. No one will buy a new, white, house in Spain if it is marketed in a dull, boring way.

These companies only have one or two European offices, but usually have an additional office in Spain, or work closely with a Spanish associate. The selling process is again to visit Spain, probably on an inspection flight. Time is more flexible, but the consumer's choice may be slightly more limited.

A word of warning. With such good value for money a Spanish property is a bargain, but it is no bargain if the dream home has been built on someone else's land, or in a protected area, or is being sold by someone who is not the rightful owner. In 1973 the Federation of Overseas Property Developers, Agents and Consultants was formed and is now the UK's primary overseas property organisation. Similar professional organisations exist in other European countries. A trouble free transaction starts here.

THE SPANISH ESTATE AGENT – *INMOBILIARIA*

It would be unusual for an estate agent of Spanish nationality to be at a property exhibition in Europe. In tandem with a European colleague perhaps, but not in isolation. They have a curious name – *inmobiliaria*, a word almost suggesting that 'a person does not move'. Yet in Spain these people are very common – small local estate agents who know their patch well, concentrating mainly on resale properties. They need not be Spanish – and indeed many are German, Scandinavian or British.

It is a good idea to deal with a registered estate agent. In Spain they belong to the Agente de Propiedad Inmobiliaria, have a certificate of registration and an identification number. They can be sued if anything goes wrong. Dealing with such a registered business gives the purchaser more security and confidence.

There are always stories in Spain of people losing their life savings because they have dealt with an unscrupulous estate agent. They may have bought a house only to discover the person selling it did not own it in the first place. The only real way to avoid this is to deal with a registered agent whose number should be on a sign outside the office, or on a window display, or on the exterior of the building. Grandiose marketing names mean nothing, its the number that counts.

Additional services offered by these companies are limited, their main preoccupation being the selling of property. One of the most difficult situations facing a newcomer to Spain occurs in the first few days of moving into a new property when they are trying to cope with a multitude of issues. Someone offering help is often welcome but regrettably it is not generally an *inmobiliaria*.

VIEWING OVER THE WEB

If you are buying a home in Spain, using the internet to find a property will save time and money. There are now plenty of websites advertising Spanish property which can be viewed from the comfort of home. Many agents maintain individual sites which can be found through internet search engines, and more are signing onto property portals for advertising.

One Spanish company has details of more than 100,000

properties from 550 agents. It offers virtual reality tours that give a true impression of the property.

Another alternative is to visit websites that specialise in private sales. Direct sales are more common in Spain than in other European countries. Buyers often prefer dealing with owners rather than agents because they trust owners more and they have a better knowledge of the property. The sales price too will not be inflated by the agent's commission.

UNDERSTANDING ADVERTISEMENTS

When an advertisement appears in a newspaper it has a few words of description, accompanied by a photograph. It is often 'word art' to describe a home in as few abbreviated words as possible. However, an additional complexity in Spain is the language barrier: difficult enough at the best of times, but in the abbreviated form, even more obtuse.

Example 1 – a standard description

Playa Flamenca Al Andalus 702. Delightful 2 year old duplex. Immaculate condition. Partly furnished. End plot. 3 beds, 2 bathrooms, large lounge, fitted kitchen, balcony, solarium, 82 sq meters. Colourful mature gardens, car parking and communal swimming pool. Price . . . Tele . . .

Taken from the property section of an English language edition weekly newspaper this advertisement describes the house adequately. Note the use of square metres to specify the size. A solarium is a top floor sun terrace.

Example 2 – a Spanish language description

Chalet, tres dormitories, dos banos, piscina, 80 sq metres, situada Playa Rio, Precio . . . Tele . . .

This example is very similar to the previous one, but in Spanish. Translation is not difficult. It means 'A detached house, with 3 bedrooms, 2 bathrooms, private swimming pool, 80 sq metres, situated in Playa Rio'. Again the size is quoted which enables the price per square metre to be calculated.

Example 3 – detached, luxury house

Chalet Adosado aguas nuevas, parcela 425 M2. Const 125 M2, gran salon con chimenea, concina indep con galeria. 3 dor, 2 banos. Porche, solarium, garaje 50 M2, a estreenar lujo. Pricio . . . Tele . . .

An altogether more imposing house set in its own grounds: 425 M2 is again the size, this time of the plot. It has heating and many extras. *Estreenar lujo* means a luxury structure. Taken from a newspaper the advert is too abbreviated and does not reflect adequately the true nature of this property.

SUMMARY

• Reading newspapers and going to property exhibitions moves the search for a home in the sun to an 'active project'.

• Before going to an exhibition clear objectives need to be set.

• International property companies tend to concentrate on new houses, *inmobiliarias* concentrate on resale property and traditional estate agents on both.

• Try to deal with agents who are professionally recognised. Do not be overwhelmed by grandiose marketing titles that may carry no accreditation.

• Viewing can be by inspection flight, a holiday and – considered to be the best – a short term rental in the area of your choice.

- Viewing over the web can save time and effort.

- Advertisements or descriptions of a property should always carry details of the price and the size in square metres. This enables a price per square metre of different properties to be compared.

4

What and Where to Buy

HOUSE NAMES AND THEIR DESCRIPTION

New houses can have names such as Fiesta, Coral, Carmen, Fortuna, Bellavista, Alba, Neptuno, Perla and Rosa, to name but a few. In agents' literature these properties usually have a photograph, a plan drawing, a location indicator and a very brief description. The size of the plot, the constructed area, room sizes and the size of the solarium and terrace are all quoted in square metres. The price is stated, but usually on a separate sheet, as it is subject to change. Surprisingly, the original marketing names are retained for many years.

We have grown accustomed to property descriptions such as apartment, terrace, town house, semi detached, detached and bungalow. In Spain property descriptions have to cross several different languages, losing some of their meaning in the process. The main descriptive terms are usually: apartment, linked (another name for terraced), town house, duplex, corner duplex, corner bungalow, semi detached, and detached (which includes bungalow). The word 'villa' is often used to describe a 'house'. The words 'chalet style' indicate a porch with a roof overhang.

In house building terminology, the phrase 'duplex' means a house with an internal staircase built on two levels and a corner duplex is a grouping of four houses, each on two floors, joined together in a rectangle. Similarly a corner bungalow is a grouping of four single storey houses joined in a rectangle. Occasionally a block of homes are built together comprising six, eight or even twelve units, in all different sizes and configurations. Although they are known by their individual names, they are mainly apartments.

THE BUILDING SPECIFICATION

A modern Spanish house is built to a high specification with little wood used in its construction. It is a strong property, of concrete and brick, which tends to carry sound easily. This noisy characteristic is at its worst in apartments, terraced and corner duplex constructions where sound travels easily through the concrete floors. Water pipes are set unobtrusively in the walls which may cause problems should they leak. A major property selling feature is achieved by having a low maintaince finish on both inside and outside walls.

Although they may vary in different parts of the country, Spanish houses are designed to achieve coolness in summer, partly through the use of window shutters to block out the hot summer sunlight. Let's look at a typical, new property specification.

- Tiling in the kitchen from floor to ceiling.
- Tiling in the bathrooms from floor to ceiling.
- Ceramic floor tiles throughout the property.
- Brick masonry work with air gap insulation.
- Exterior low maintenance wall finish in cement roughcast or small marble chippings.
- Sloping roofs made with partitions forming the slope, ceramic bricks and cement mortar finish with curved roof tiles.
- Flat terraces fitted with ceramic terrace tiles.
- Shutters on windows.
- Interior walls to be finished in white low maintenance plastic paint, known as Gotele style.
- Fitted kitchen units (top and bottom), worktops, stainless steel sink. Electric points for cooker, fan extractor, fridge and washing machine.
- Interior carpentry lacquered to natural colours with exterior door to 40 mm thickness and interior doors to 35 mm thickness.

- Copper plumbing installation with hot and cold. National sanitary fitments of a high standard. Sewerage pipes of PVC set in concrete.
- Reinforced foundations.
- Internal cabling for telephone and television
- Optional extras can include more electrical points, heating or air conditioning and security grilles on all windows and doors.

CONSIDERING THE PROS AND CONS OF EACH HOUSE TYPE

Apartment

An apartment offers easy living in secure surroundings. In order to sell quickly apartments are always built to a high standard, with outside balconies included. Some basic economy flats exist in large cities where low cost living is a priority. Living in an apartment will probably mean Spanish neighbours. Nice people they may well be, but they tend to be noisy and have a different 'body clock' to other nationalities. Normal behaviour is to rise late, have lunch at 2.00 pm, an evening meal at 9.00 pm and go to bed at midnight or after. Family discussion is often loud, very loud, Spanish voices having the unique ability to penetrate all bricks and mortar.

Apartments are cheap, easy to resell, but often attract high community charges.

Linked, terraced and town houses

Some of the most attractive new designs are for linked and terraced houses (see Figure 5). These houses are on two levels with a third floor/roof utilised as a solarium. They too are cheap and easy to resell but lack privacy.

Town houses are obviously available new, but additionally can be older reformed traditional properties in the narrow streets of a Spanish town where car parking is a problem.

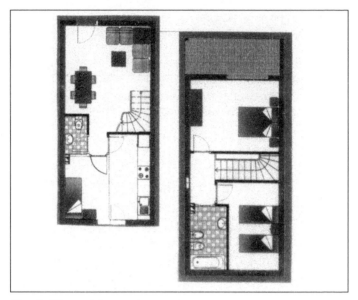

Fig. 5. Plan – A terraced property.

Corner properties

Corner housing is mostly found in duplex design but can also apply to single level homes (see Figure 6). It is a cheap form of building having fewer external walls. Services, although individual to each home, do have some common elements. Corner duplexes are noisy, but their main function is holiday homes, with neighbours rarely meeting.

Detached

These properties offer privacy at the expense of security. They can be expensive. Built to an individual design (see Figure 7) they are sometimes perched precariously on cutaway hillsides, so much so that insurance companies can charge a premium. · Windswept plots make dust a perpetual irritant. Even with some

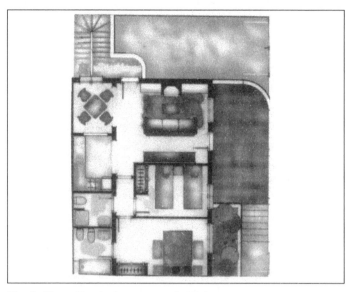

Fig. 6. Plan – Two bedroom corner bungalow.

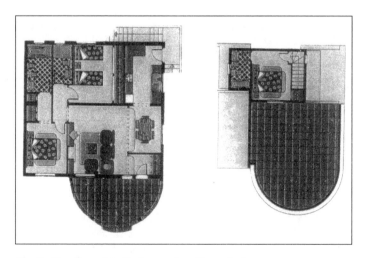

Fig. 7. Two floor detached property with a solarium.

disadvantages a detached property is desirable, particularly one that overlooks the sea or the mountains or even a lush green golf course.

Traditional homes

So far we have looked at relatively new properties. Older Spanish properties exist. In most cases they have been modernised or rebuilt. This is called a reformed house. In the country they are called *fincas*. In the town they are obviously called town houses. A reformed town house is in many respects an ideal property since it gives easy access to the town with the benefits of living in new modern surroundings.

But the classic is a *finca rustica*, usually located in the country. It is where dreams are made. It can be a labour of love, with considerable skill, determination and money required in order to rebuild an old crumbling building into a individual, personalised property of pride and charm. Renovating a property, or indeed maintaining it, demands very good DIY skills. Living in one needs patience, a degree of tolerance and some enthusiasm to deal with everyday problems.

LIVING IN URBANISATIONS AND COMMUNITIES

Urbanisations

Life on an urbanisation is popular whatever the type of house. Sitting by the swimming pool meeting new continental friends, passing the time of day with a glass of wine in hand is an agreeable way of life. Little Spanish is spoken. Sharing experiences bonds the community together. Informal groupings take place. Golfing partners come together. Coffee mornings just happen. Family problems are shared. The siesta is forgotten as people assemble in the local bar to escape the searing heat of the afternoon sun. Life is easy. However, it is very important for

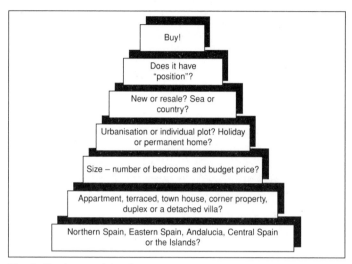

Fig. 8. Buying considerations.

mind and body to stay active or a slow soporific mental decline will occur.

Behaviour standards need to be set. An urbanisation is a community by itself where the level is set by the standard of the lowest.

Community property

What is a community property? The answer is one that involves homes with a shared element. An example would be apartments, or a grouping of individual homes. Urbanisations have a shared element in the swimming pool or gardens. Apartments have a shared element in the lift. Detached properties may have a common access road.

The cost of maintaining these elements is shared between the owners. The most expensive shared element is normally the swimming pool, followed by gardens and satellite TV. Spanish council services are limited, with elements such as street cleaning being part of the community costs.

The *communidad de propietarios* can be run by an independent company on behalf of the owners or, in a well organised community, by the owners themselves. Germans have a talent for this, the Spanish an eye for detail and the Scandinavians are laid back. The British and Irish seem happy to leave it to others.

Annual meetings are certainly long and argumentative, often bitter, as many nationalities, resident and non-resident, seek to have a voice. There is a Spanish law that surrounds these communities. As you would expect, it is quite complex. It is called The Law of Horizontal Property.

NEW OR RESALE?

When moving to Spain most people prefer to buy a new property. It is rather like buying a car. Why buy second hand if you can buy new? A resale property is slightly more expensive, after all drives have been laid, gardens are mature and it often comes with furniture and fittings. A resale property built within the last ten years may still carry a guarantee. It can be good value. In some, now overdeveloped, parts of Spain, it is the only type of property available.

Mention should be made of Spain's peculiar debt laws where the debt is on the property and not the person. Any outstanding debt occurred by the old owner is automatically carried over to a new owner. The complexities of this are explained later.

LIVING BY THE SEA OR IN THE COUNTRY

By the sea

This is a pleasant experience with cool afternoon breezes taking the sting out of the searing summer heat. But nearly all Mediterranean towns are tourist areas. In July and August with temperatures always in excess of 30 degrees, people pour in on package holidays. Spaniards too have their summer holiday then, as they rush to the coast in their thousands from the torrid heat of the big cities. For two frustrating months the beaches are packed, the roads jammed, car parks full and tempers frayed.

Mention should be made of Spain's 'Law of the Coasts', which empowers local authorities to restrict the number, height and density of buildings within 100 metres of the high water mark and to establish a zone of influence as far inward as one kilometre. Properties continue to be built near beaches as they comply with the regulations. They do, however, command a hefty premium for their position, the price only being reduced with a high density building design.

In the country

Living in the country has many attractions. Living in the country is living in the real Spain. It is peaceful with privacy assured. Neighbours, although far apart, are normally friendly. Large plots of land enable the growing of oranges, lemons, olives or almonds. Some of these properties have no electricity, no water, no sewage disposal, no gas and no telephone. All these facilities can be compensated for by other means. Electricity can be supplied by a generator and batteries, or by solar panels. Water can be delivered by tanker. A septic tank takes care of sewage. Bottles supply the gas. Communication can be by mobile or radio telephone.

WHICH DIRECTION?

There is a bay at Calpe with a hilly headland jutting out eastwards to sea. Houses have been built on this hill. They face north. They are cold houses as they get little direct sun.

Individual houses, a terraced row, or apartments facing north or north east all suffer from the same fate – little sun in the winter months and consequently quite cold interiors. These properties are sold, not by referring to any direction, but by saying 'Cool in summer'. For year round living it is better to choose a property facing south. For a summer holiday home it is not so important.

A compass is a handy tool to take when viewing property for direction is rarely stated in agents' literature. When new, north facing properties are the last to sell, often attracting discounts or special offers in order to complete the transaction.

OPTIONAL EXTRAS

Security

Security can be a problem. A property must be secure at all times particularly when the owner is absent. The most effective method of securing a property is to fit metal grilles (*rejas*) to external doors and windows. Alternative alarm systems are available, usually linked to a central telephone control point in Madrid. But grilles are the most popular, being available in many decorative designs. In truth this is not really an optional extra. For peace of mind it is a necessity.

Heating and air conditioning

Is heating, or air conditioning, or both, really necessary? The answer, as one would expect, depends on the exact area.

Let us start with the Costa Blanca, after all it does carry that prestigious recommendation from the World Health Organisation. Portable gas or electric heaters, over a 12 week winter period, to take the chill off rooms is all that is necessary. Similarly, fans to move the air around in summer will suffice. It has to be said, however, that more and more people are installing central heating and air conditioning as comfort levels are obviously increased by an all-in-one system. Some new homes are built with this installed, but it is not strictly necessary.

Appropriate precautions for the Costa Blanca also apply equally to the Costa del Sol, the Canaries and the Balearic Islands.

Moving north and inland some form of heating system is
necessary. Northern Spain requires full central heating. The
centre of the country, including inland Andalucia, needs all the
aids for comfortable living that can be mustered with heating
and air conditioning a necessity.

Swimming pool

With so many communal pools around, a private swimming
pool is a luxury and not a necessity. Each small village has its
own municipal pool. Perhaps if one lived in the country, a pool
to help cool off would be desirable. But water in Spain is
precious. The unit cost increases with consumption, so pool
owners pay hefty charges.

Garden

A garden completes a home. Residents should have a full garden
laid out with palm trees and colourful hibiscus shrubs. Non
residents require a maintenance-free environment, laying out the
garden to paving stones, chippings and the occasional water-
thrifty shrub. Green lawns are rarely seen, such is the expense
and difficulty of upkeep.

THE MAGICAL HOUSING INGREDIENT – POSITION

What do we really want when buying a house?

Is it a property close to the sea, overlooking a golf course,
with easy access to the countryside, a town, and an airport? Is it
to be new, white, set in a large plot of land? Do restaurants,
pubs, hospitals, doctors and dentists have to be close by? Are
neighbours only to be British, Irish and the rather pleasant
Dutch? Should crime be non-existent?

No, not really! What we do is to set a number of priorities
which are usually the price, the number of bedrooms, the type of
house and the location. Then we look for Position.

The three Ps beloved by property consultants are Position, Position and Position. It is that little magic that makes a property unique and easy to sell.

- It is no good buying a large detached property surrounded by cheap flats. It will just lose value.

- A property at the end of a street, facing a commercial centre, will suffer the same fate.

- A property in the middle of a row of similar houses has nothing to commend it. Future resale values are dependent on the general ambience of the area.

- Position is location. A sea view perhaps. Overlooking orange and lemon groves. Close to a pine filled ravine. At the edge of purple hills. Next to a marina. Looking over lush green fairways.

- More simply it can be exotic gardens or a house that has obviously been well loved and cared for.

- Position is that little bit extra making a property highly desirable – and probably that little bit more expensive.

CASE STUDY – PURCHASING

Heather and Peter were both professional people in their 50s. The children had left home. They had decided to buy a holiday home in the sun which could, at a later date, be used as a retirement home. They attended a large international property exhibition at Brighton. Although they considered Cyprus they settled for Spain because it was closer and could be reached by car.

Most of the exhibitors seemed to be talking about new properties on the Costa Blanca. One was able to answer their questions knowledgably and provided them with several

---

options and numerous coloured brochures. After a few days' consideration they booked an inspection flight.

They were both acutely aware of the subtle selling pressures. Before leaving they received a phone call, 'Just to remind you to have the ten per cent deposit ready. A cheque will do.' They were met at the airport, put up in a good hotel, were wined and dined and efficiently escorted everywhere.

As well as looking at property, their guide stopped frequently at sandy bays, taking them to lunch at the marina and golf club restaurants, all with the intention of showing the general ambience of the area to its best advantage.

'We are not here to sell you anything, just to show you around, give the facts,' said the guide. Later, when discussing the special offers of cars, discounts and furniture packs, out popped the question 'What is your budget?'

Heather and Peter were fully aware that an inspection trip was in fact a code name for a buying trip. They felt under pressure to buy, but equally in control of the situation, having previously done considerable homework on the area itself. They were impressed with what they saw, were delighted at some of the properties and paid a ten per cent non returnable deposit for a new corner duplex to be completed in 12 months' time.

WHAT DO PEOPLE BUY?

People moving to Spain for the first time often purchase a new property sold by an international property company of some repute, giving a sense of security in a country where the customs and laws are unfamiliar to the purchaser. There may well be a 12-month wait for the property to be built, which can be to standard or individual design. With the complex legal procedures in Spain this type of purchase is the simplest, with no debt issues to worry about. The property company is also to hand to deal with any outstanding problems.

In some parts of the country a resale property is the most common purchase. Slightly older properties, in mature areas where new buildings are not so prevalent, are an attractive proposition to many. The legal procedures are slightly more complex and quite different from those experienced during the purchase of a completely new property.

Discerning buyers look for something unique. They are in the minority. They know the country well. They understand its culture, customs and procedures. They may have lived in Spain for a few years or be buying a second house inland from the Costas. Buying a plot of land, a ruin for renovation, a property under construction, or perhaps building your own house are all possible options. These combinations do, however, require a good understanding of Spain's legal procedures.

SUMMARY

- House descriptions are less well defined in Spain. They lose some meaning as they cross language barriers.

- A normal house specification is mainly of brick and concrete construction. It can be noisy. A principle of design is 'for the house to be kept cool in summer'.

- The many different house types and locations offer the customer a bewildering choice. What style? New or resale? By the sea or inland?

- A viewing checklist should include a compass.

- Security is not an optional extra. Have grilles built into the house.

- Concentrate on location, price and the number of bedrooms.

- Make a budgetary allowance for the extra special ingredient of 'position'.

5

The People Involved

THE BUILDER

Given the amount of construction taking place in Spain one
could be forgiven for thinking it was the country's major
industry. Motorways are still being built, linking major
Mediterranean cities to the capital Madrid. Distribution depots
owned by companies in Europe, the USA and Spain are
springing up at major road junctions. In cities and along coastal
strips, hotels, apartments and houses continue to be built.
Factories, assisted by EU grants, are being erected too, thus
maintaining Spain's industrial growth.

Construction is big business. It is highly skilled. There is a
shortage of skilled tradesmen, and many travel from the more
remote parts of Spain to work on the coastal developments.

What of the house builder? Broadly there are three types.

- A large builder accustomed to building 500 houses or one
  large apartment block per year. He may be in partnership
  with a developer but his main business preoccupation is with
  planning, finance and management. The actual building work
  is carried out by a team of site managers. He will rarely get
  involved in sales or marketing, appointing several multi-
  lingual agents to perform this task. Sometimes, however, he
  will sell direct to the public, cutting out agents and their
  commissions.

- A medium sized builder constructing 30 to 50 units per year.
  A row of terraced houses or individually designed properties
  cut into the hillside are examples of the scale of his

71

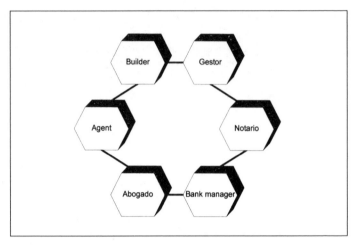

Fig. 9. *Los hombres grandes* of the buying process.

operation. The builder himself would be on site supervising the day to day activities but he too would probably appoint agents to carry out sales and marketing.

- A small builder, who may be Spanish or originally from Ireland, Britain or Germany, who will at the most be engaged in house restoration, or at a minimum engaged in laying garden patios or building dividing walls. He will carry out all the work personally.

They are all highly skilled individuals. Employees will be treated firmly but benevolently, as befits an industry with a labour shortage. Starting work at 8.00 am and finishing at about 6.00 pm they will have breakfast at 10.00 am and a longer break for lunch at 2.00 pm – complete with the customary bottle of red wine which will be taken, or left, much as a Northern European would treat a glass of water.

Bankruptcy insurance policy

All builders should have an insurance policy to cover the possibility of going bankrupt before completing the property. The number and details of this policy should be stated in the purchase contract, but often is not, giving rise to the clear suspicion that insurance may not have been arranged.

It is desirable to have the security of this insurance policy. But in Spain there is always a need to be pragmatic. For an additional safeguard, stage payments should be in line with building progress. After all, that is precisely the reason for stage payments. Making the stage payments according to the building progress is the best insurance policy.

Strangely it is small builders who are more likely to go bankrupt, yet their work is more tightly monitored by the owner. The larger builders have bank managers checking their cash flow.

The financial consequences of a builder going bankrupt are clear, but it is also the time delays while an alternative builder is found, which causes additional frustration.

THE AGENT

A good agent
An agent is the focal point of buying. In previous chapters emphasis was laid on the following key issues:

- A good agent is one who can offer a wide variety of properties for sale.

- Greater security is offered by dealing with an agent who is professionally qualified or belongs to a professional organisation.

- For first time buyers, uncertain of the laws and customs of the country, a good agent will give additional assistance during the difficult moving-in stage.

But we need to go back, to examine the profession of the agent. They may be called estate agents, real estate agents, property companies or by the Spanish term *inmobiliaria*. They may work alone or have their offices linked across Europe by the internet. But horror stories about buying Spanish properties usually start here with the agent. Having said that most agents, of whatever nationality, are both registered and honest. They seek to make a high commission, on the sale of good properties, making both buyer and seller happy. In theory they work for the seller. In practice they work for themselves.

Charges

Agents dealing in Spanish property do take a high commission. The lowest start at around three per cent but the average is ten per cent. When selling a *finca* it can be 25 per cent. How do they justify such exorbitant charges? Their answer is ambiguous, making reference to high advertising costs, commissions due in two countries and complex transactions involving different nationalities. In truth it is simply a seller's market with demand outstripping supply, causing many people to enter the lucrative business of house selling.

In the small, very popular town of Javea there are over 100 estate agents. Why? With house prices at 400,000 Euros, each agent only has to sell around six properties per year to make an extremely comfortable living. It is often the case, in the final stages of house price negotiation, that the agent's commission itself may well be reviewed downwards. Very few agents in Spain operate on an exclusive basis and rarely expect to do so. It is quite common to find several agents selling the same property. Since their commissions may differ, so ironically may the house price.

New properties

The commission rate for selling a new house on behalf of a

builder is usually fixed at around ten per cent. If a number of agents are selling the same properties they may compete with one another, discounting their commission by offering furniture packages to prospective purchasers.

Resale properties

A different commission structure operates for the sale of a second-hand property, commonly termed a resale property. In some cases the agent operates on a fixed commission, but it is more customary for the following arrangement:

- The agent asks the seller the price he wishes for the property.

- He advertises and negotiates the sale of the property at another, higher price.

- The difference between the two prices is the agent's commission, which is rarely less than 10 per cent, more likely to be 15 per cent and can in special cases reach 25 per cent.

- This pricing structure gives rise to considerably animosity. It is compounded when buyer and seller seldom meet, possibly creating an atmosphere of mistrust in relation to the commercial motives of the agent.

- It is a commonly held view that, when selling a resale property in Spain, it is only the agent who gets rich. It certainly breeds agents who ensure:

    – the buyer pays a high price
    – the seller gets a low price
    – the agent gains a high commission.

Bogus agents

Property buyers in many European countries are carefully protected during a major financial transaction. They are even protected from their own mistakes by the right to withdraw from an agreement for up to several weeks after signing the appropriate contract. They should be a little bit more wary in Spain where the regulation of conveyancing is only carried out at the final stages by the *notario*, a representative of the Spanish government.

Who are the people who give rise to the horror stories? It is the British who trick the British, the Germans who trick the Germans, the Scandinavians who trick the Scandinavians and so on. Why? It is the language issue once again. Someone talking to you in your own language will sound more plausible, particularly someone who has already gained your confidence and understanding. It is unlikely that you would be tricked by someone of another nationality.

Five methods of thwarting bogus agents

- Ensure that any money, deposit or stage payment, goes to a blocked account where no party can get at it until the sale is completed. The agent will want the deposit paid to him in cash. But it is not his house! It should be paid to the owner. Only a blocked account settles the argument.

- Use a Spanish lawyer when buying Spanish property. Do not use a legal expert in your own country to check out the legal documents in another country. Would you use a German lawyer to check British conveyencing or vice versa? No. Why should it be different in Spain?

- Take care with the deposit. Make absolutely certain you are fully aware whether the deposit is returnable or non-returnable in the event of failing to complete the transaction.

Or alternatively ask the number of days' grace in which you can change your mind. Do not accept the agent's word – ask to see the agreement in writing.

- The payment of a deposit is the first of the financial and legal steps in buying a property. It must be linked to a contract. The deposit is normally up to ten per cent, payable in cash, cheque or banker's draft to the agent or the seller.

- The contract can be between the agent and the purchaser, the builder and the purchaser or drawn up between the seller and purchaser with the help of a solicitor. All are valid. The key factor is the content of the contract itself.

THE *ABOGADO* (SOLICITOR)

Finding a good *abogado* is not an easy matter. They do not advertise in newspapers. They have signs outside the office door, but these are discreet indicators of their presence rather than advertising mechanisms. It is word of mouth that results in the appointment of a good *abogado*.

It may well be the agent who recommends an *abogado*. It could be the bank manager or a friend. Either way, there are many people engaged in this highly respected profession, admired for their ability to deal with Spanish law, where complex legal, procedural and administrative issues tend to bog down matters.

Sitting in modern offices, working long hours and charging moderate fees, is not everyone's idea of fun. Some larger offices have multi-lingual Scandinavian staff who seem to speak English with American accents. It is better if your legal representative speaks your mother tongue. Understanding complex financial arrangements becomes so much easier.

It is important to remember that the appointment of a legal representative is principally to protect the buyer. The agent is working for the seller. As with many other aspects of daily life, it is a system of checks and balances. But let us be clear at the outset. The Spanish system of house conveyancing is different. You are not dealing with solicitors who draw up and exchange contracts on completion. The final lynch-pin of the Spanish system is the *notario*.

So what does the *abogado* do? They can:

- Draw up a contract should he be asked to do so.

- Complete the conveyancing of property at around three per cent of the purchase price excluding the major property tax currently charged at seven per cent.

- Provide help and guidance on legal matters, principally the content of the contract and payment methods.

- Make arrangements to obtain and receive Power of Attorney.

- Obtain an NIE number so that a client's personal identification is by name and also number. An NIE number is required for house purchase, car ownership and for the payment of taxes (see Chapter 9).

- Make arrangements for signing the *escritura* and final property payments (see Chapter 9).

- Assist with fiscal representation, administration and the drawing up of wills if asked.

Power of Attorney

This simple mechanism is useful if the purchaser cannot be in Spain when the legal paperwork requires completion. If the property is in joint names and one person cannot attend, then a Power of Attorney is essential. People on holiday can avoid weary queues at the *notario* by delegating the Power of Attorney to a legal representative.

A Special Power of Attorney can only deal with the buying or selling of property. A General Power of Attorney can deal with almost anything but is likely to embrace loans and mortgages.

To draw up a Power of Attorney, visit the local notary's office, with passport, and details of who the Power of Attorney is 'for' and who it is given 'to', together with a payment of approximately 50 Euros. A few days later the document will be ready for signature.

If a Power of Attorney is required it does make sense to have it drawn up at the onset of a purchase, but of course it is possible to conclude such an authorisation at any time. It is even possible to draw up a Power of Attorney without leaving home as the Spanish Consulate in any country can prepare one. Signing a Power of Attorney in a Spanish Consulate is the same as if it had been signed in Spain.

THE BANK MANAGER

Walking down the *calle mayor* (high street) of any Spanish town the names of many banks will be prominent. Caja Madrid, Caja Murcia, Banco de Santander, Banco Bilbao Vizcaya Argentaria (BBVA) are a few examples which demonstrate the ability of each city to spawn its own bank. Incidentally the word *caja* means bank or till.

Banking in Spain is fragmented. There are about 150 different banks serving different markets and with different functions. Clearing banks, savings banks, lending banks, cooperative banks and some foreign banks of French, German or British parentage compete on an equal footing. These banks have many, many branches but care is required as naturally some of the smaller outlets do not offer a full range of services.

But banking is changing. Frequent takeovers or amalgamations occur as these organisations seek national coverage for their products changing strategy from their historic regional roots.

What bank?

A bank may be recommended by the agent, the *abogado* or be linked with a bank back home. It is unlikely to be of Irish or British parentage since they are few in number. German banks have a strong presence. Here are some recommended criteria for selecting a bank:

- Some staff, preferably the manager, should speak English.

- The branch should be relatively close to the new property.

- In order to have access to major services such as mortgages and investments, the bank should be a major player in the Spanish marketplace.

- Money transferred into Spain for the purchase of a property will come through the clearing bank system. The home bank and the Spanish bank should both be main branches to prevent delays in money transfer.

Make no mistake, while Spanish banking has some complicated procedures, it is reasonably efficient, usually staffed by friendly, hard working, multi-lingual people capable of offering the customer some of the most up to date services including telephone, TV interactive and internet banking.

Credit or debit plastic cards are accepted for the purchase of consumer goods but sometimes only with some other form of identification containing a photograph, such as a passport or ID card. The principal use of plastic cards is to obtain cash, at a small charge, from an ATM (hole in the wall cash dispenser) of which there are many.

Strategic and offshore banking

The use of two accounts, one in your home country and one in

Spain, should be enough for most needs. The transfer of money between the two is straightforward particularly if in Euros. For transfers between sterling and Euro the use of an intermediate link, such as that provided by TAPS (Bank of Scotland electronic money transfer system), is cost effective.

Offshore banking has some advantages for investments and tax free savings. The EU is trying to close such loopholes. Since Gibraltar is so close to the Costa del Sol it is still possible to bank offshore. Many offshore current accounts offer a cash or credit withdrawal world wide. However, a charge of 2.25 per cent for exchange rates and 1.5 per cent per withdrawal makes confidential offshore banking expensive.

Non residents' certificate

There are no financial exchange controls in Spain. The Euro is the dominant currency. A property is best paid for by a banker's order in Euros but sensible alternative methods are permissible. The key principle of this financial transaction is to have it documented within Spain through the buyer's bank.

The financial transaction can be completed outside Spain. For example the money can be transferred from the buyer's account in Edinburgh to the seller's account in Dublin. But to do this a 'Certificate of Non-Residence' is required. It is issued in Spain by the Ministry of Interior and helps the Spanish tax man keep track of where the money comes from and goes to. This will take time; without it the notary will not approve the purchase.

The Euro

Euro coins and notes have been circulating in EU member countries from January 2002. The much loved Peseta has now gone, held only in fond memories. At its launch the Euro instantly devalued but recently it has strengthened against Europe's other major currency, Sterling, and equally against the mighty Dollar, Which currency is weak or strong is a matter of speculation. Currency fluctuations emphasise a view that a Spanish property owner is better to earn, borrow or repay money on one currency be it the Pound, Dollar or Euro. But to earn and repay in one currency, is also advantageous.

The relationship between the Pound and the Euro is still floating. In the first few years it has fluctuated by only 3%. In the case of the Dollar the variation has been slightly greater. The following formulae, although not strictly accurate, is a good guide for everyday purposes.

6 Dollars = 6 Euros = 4 British Pounds = 1000 old pesetas

Mortgage facilities

Need a mortgage? The Spanish bank is a provider. Need a short term bridging loan? Forget it. These two statements demonstrate a difference in attitude towards borrowing money. A loan is for business, a mortgage for home finance with the two kept strictly separate. There are no building societies or their equivalent in Spain with the exception of a few based in Gibraltar. Banks therefore have a captive market for the provision of home finance. The criteria for a mortgage are quite familiar:

- The earnings of one or both purchasers are taken into account.

- The property is valued, not at market value, but at a rebuild cost per square metre.

- The maximum mortgage for a non-resident is around 60 per cent of the valuation. The maximum for a resident around 80 per cent.

- A combination of a low valuation based on rebuilding cost and not market value, and a low mortgage based on that valuation, means the actual mortgage can be as low as 40 per cent of the market price of the property.

- Mortgages are easily concluded but banks take very little risk in granting them.

CASE STUDY – OPENING A BANK ACCOUNT

Peter has decided to open a bank account. He stands in a long, slow moving, patient queue of many nationalities. Sometime later it is his turn.

'Hola, I wish to open a current account.'

'OK Senor, no problem. I speak English. Can I have your passport please? Can you fill in the form please?'

Ten minutes later, 'Here is the form completed'.

The banking assistant examines the form. 'Bien, very good. Firma aqui, por favor (sign here please).'

'Firma again.'

'Here is your passport returned and a copy of our terms.'

'Thank you. When do I get the cheque book and credit card?'

'The cheque book in five days. Remember you have opened a current account with no overdraft facilities. Please also remember it is not a credit card, only a debit card. It will be ready in about 20 days, Senor.'

'That's a bit long. What do I do in the meantime?'

A pause, a shrug of the shoulders, 'Cash, Senor, cash, or if you do not like cash, a banker's order.'

'You will send them on to my home address?'

'Oh no Senor, you collect here at the bank. The post, it is not reliable. You must collect it.'

And so a bank account is opened. The new cheque book has the words printed at the top, '*Cuenta en Euros de no Residente*'. This indicates the Spanish banking system distinguishes residents from non-residents for tax purposes.

THE *NOTARIO*

In Spain all deeds for properties are drawn up by Public Notaries who are appointed by the Government. They are qualified lawyers who have additionally studied to become notaries. They are very important people in the Spanish community, responsible for legalising many documents including the Power of Attorney, drawing up wills, certifying copies of passports, and most importantly approving the deed of a property, known in Spain as the *escritura*.

The *escritura* is signed and witnessed by the *notario* in the presence of the seller(s) and the purchaser(s) unless any party has utilised the Power of Attorney to excuse their own presence. The *notario*'s duty is to :

- Check the name of the title holder and whether there are any charges or encumbrances against the property.
- Check the contents of the *escritura*.
- Ensure the *escritura* is read to the purchaser(s) prior to signing.
- Check that both parties have been advised of their legal obligations.
- Certify the *escritura* has been signed and the money paid.

The *notario* represents the State. He does not guarantee or verify statements or check the contractual terms. He protects the interests of the buyer or seller by pointing out any pitfalls, by offering advice on legal points and volunteering information. Although some do, a *notario* is not expected to speak any language other than his native tongue or to explain the complexities of Spanish law.

The document

The end product of a visit to the *notario* is the *escritura*. It is a hard backed copy of the deed which is covered in official stamps, signatures and writing. It is typed on thick, numbered paper. It is an impressive document produced to a standard format. All *escrituras* start with the date, the name of the *notario* and the protocol number which are effectively the filing references should another copy be required.

THE GESTOR

A *gestor* is a registered agent dealing with government departments and acts as an intermediary between Spanish officialdom and the general public. It says much about the Spanish way of life that such a person is necessary to deal with its wearisome bureaucracy.

A *gestor* is a well respected occupation. They are competent, highly qualified administrators whose fees are somewhat less than those of the *abogado*.

What do they do? For the Spanish they simply deal with the complicated mass of paperwork. For foreigners they do the same, in a country where the language barrier, a new culture and different procedures cause additional problems. The tasks covered by the *gestor* are mainly:

- payment of income and wealth taxes
- application for residency
- entry into the Spanish health system
- dealing with the payment of car tax, car transfer tax and other car related matters
- if required, help in setting up new businesses.

In all probability a new house owner will not require the services of a *gestor* until after the house conveyancing is completed. Up to this time he will be best serviced by the advice of the *abogado*.

Of course, as a new resident's knowledge increases with time, some of the day to day administration of minor items can be accomplished personally.

CHECKING DEBTS

Spain's debt laws carry a property debt over to the new owner. Who checks these debts? What are these debts? A check has to be made to ensure there are no encumbrances on the property such as mortgages or loans, or outstanding debts such as local taxes and community charges, and that services bills have been paid in full. The following is a process for checking this:

- A copy of the *nota simple* (see Chapter 6 for a full explanation of this) will tell if there are any mortgages or loans against the property. The seller is not trusted to pay off this debt, so it must be paid off before signing the *escritura*. With a mortgaged property the organisation redeeming the mortgage is present in the *notario*'s office to receive their money.

- Enquire at the town hall to see if there are any unpaid local taxes (see Chapter 12).

- Enquire through the Community of Owners, or their management company, to ascertain all community charges have been paid.

- Check receipts provided by the seller that all bills for electricity, water, telephone and gas have been paid.

A first time buyer probably does not have the time or local knowledge to carry out these checks. A good agent should do this. As we have seen, a notary will carry out some of these checks. An *abogado* will do a fine job as his professional reputation is at risk. But a bank manager issuing a mortgage will do it even better since the bank's money is at risk. Some banks appoint third party organisations to carry out these checks on their behalf.

Remember, all unpaid debts on a property are inherited by the buyer.

AVOIDING PROBLEMS

Problems associated with purchasing a property abroad have

been highlighted many times in the popular press. From a legal viewpoint Spain has not always been the safest place to buy. Most horror stories come at the start of the buying process. It is at the contract and deposit stage where things go wrong, where insufficient checks have been made, or inadequate procedures followed. Among the myriad problems experienced by buyers in Spain the most prominent are:

- unscrupulous agents
- a badly written contract
- properties bought without legal title
- issues surrounding developers and builders, lack of planning permission, companies going bankrupt, undischarged loans
- an undischarged mortgage from the previous owner
- an *escritura* which describes a property which has been altered to a degree bearing no resemblance to that described.

THE GOLDEN RULES

It cannot be emphasised too strongly that anyone planning to buy a property in Spain must take independent legal advice in a language in which they are fluent from a lawyer experienced in Spanish property law. Always deal with professionals and do not assume that because you may be dealing with a fellow countryman that the advice is better, cheaper or even unbiased.

Do not sign anything, or pay a deposit, until you have sought legal advice. Once the advice is given – take it. Do not assume it is someone dotting the I's and crossing the T's. One of the most common phrases heard in Spain is about buyers 'leaving their brains behind at the airport'. It is true! The rush to buy a dream home, or the pressurised selling trip, or even the euphoria of the moment often makes people do incredibly stupid things, literally handing over cash deposits to agents or owners with little or no security.

Again, always take legal advice.

SUMMARY

- Builders should have an insurance policy to protect against bankruptcy.

- Agents charge high commissions.

- Buyers and sellers of resale properties should be aware of the agent's commission.

- Deposits and stage payments should be made to a blocked account.

- An English speaking *abogado* is essential to the property buying process, principally for advice on contractual and payment terms.

- Spanish banking is reasonably efficient but its procedures are very different. Choose a major bank, with English speaking staff, close to your new home.

- Although mortgages are available from Spanish banks, they are relatively small.

- The *notario*, a State appointee, at the final step of the buying process offers great safeguards on legal matters.

- A *gestor* is necessary to deal with the bureaucratic way of life.

- Ensure that someone has checked the debts on a property. Spain's peculiar laws carry them over to the new owner.

- Wish to avoid problems? Always take legal advice from someone who speaks your native tongue and understands Spanish property law.

6

Understanding the Legal Documents for a New Property

ELEVEN IMPORTANT STEPS

Many people choose to buy a new property. Not one that is standing empty, completely finished, for these are rare occurrences, but a property that has yet to be built. It may be identical to a show house or built to an individual design to be constructed from a builder's plans. We will now follow this standard legal and administrative trail. It starts with the decision to purchase and follows clear steps to a conclusion in the *notario*'s office.

The steps

1. A plan of the house
2. Locating the plot
3. The agent's agreement
4. The *nota simple*
5. The contract
6. Community charges – a share of the costs
7. The *Certificado Final de la Direccion de la Obra*
8. The *Licencia de Primera Ocupacion*
9. Insurances
10. The *escritura*
11. *Registro de la Propiedad*

If a mortgage is required, or small building alterations are necessary, these will involve further steps. Obtaining a mortgage has been considered earlier in Chapter 5. The *Licencia de Obra*, a building licence, is considered in this chapter.

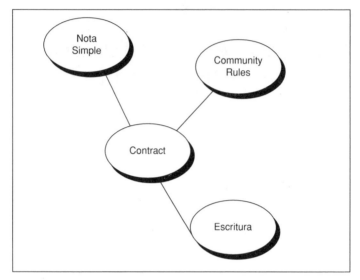

Fig. 10. The most important legal documents.

What are the important documents?

All documents are important. Failure to complete one may have serious consequences. But we must also be practical. What documents are the most important? What can we do without?

The core documentation consists of the *nota simple*, the contract, the community rules and the *escritura* (see Figure 10). Of these the **contract**, signed soon after the start of the buying process, is the most important. A good contract, correctly worded, is of benefit to both the buyer and seller. Altering a contract is almost impossible. A bad contract creates unnecessary difficulties. Reneging on a contract involves losing the deposit.

This chapter should be read alongside the following Appendices. They are all for the same property.

Appendix 1. A purchase contract issued by a builder for a new property

Appendix 2. The community rules
Appendix 3. The *escritura*

Please remember this standard procedure is only for a new property yet to be built. New properties with a fast track conveyancing procedure, resale properties, reformed houses and land purchase all follow different routes. They are considered in Chapter 10.

A PLAN OF THE HOUSE

It makes sense to have a plan of the house. Not a glossy brochure, nor a three dimensional line drawing, but an architect's plan (see Figure 11) which shows the dimensions of each floor and each room in square metres. The overall size of the house is important to determine its market price, the valuation for any mortgage, the insurance premiums and the assessment for local taxes.

LOCATING THE PLOT

It also makes sense to have a line drawing locating the plot. This is called *plan parcial*, a Spanish term meaning a plan of parcels, or plots of land, which is registered with the planning department at the local town hall. Firstly it ensures the urbanisation is legal by registering it with the town hall. Secondly it shows other adjacent developments and, most importantly, if any major roads are planned close by.

While a line drawing, supplied by the agent or builder, will suffice on most occasions, the *plan parcial*, from the *Urbanismo* department at the *Ayuntamiento* (town hall) is the approved source.

RESERVATION CONTRACT

This document represents the first step in the buying process. It

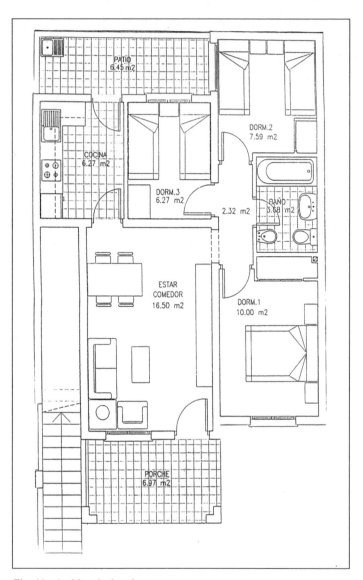

Fig. 11. Architect's drawing.

is an outline agreement to reserve the property. It should contain as a minimum the following:

- Name, address, telephone number and passport number of the purchaser.
- Name, address, telephone number and the business or personal identification of the agent.
- House type, plot number and address of the property.
- The price in Euros. This should clearly state if IVA (Value Added Tax) is included in the price.
- The reservation, deposit and payment formulae. Initially this normally involves a non-returnable deposit.
- Signed and dated by both parties.

THE *NOTA SIMPLE*

This document, which translated means a 'simple note', is issued by the Land Registry Office and is a copy of the Property Registration details (see *Registro de la Propiedad* in this chapter). For a property yet to be constructed, it will show proof that the person selling the property is the registered owner of the land and that there are no debts on the land. It should be noted that a similar methodology for existing properties is also followed, showing details of the present owner, if the property has an outstanding mortgage or loan or if it has any debts registered against it.

The significance of the document is clear. It establishes that the person building or selling the property or land is the person with the right so to do.

Obtaining a copy of the *nota simple* is straightforward. Firstly locate the Registry Office with jurisdiction over the property or land. This is not always in the nearest town or village. Secondly complete a request for information form and pay a small fee, then return in a few days to collect the *nota simple*.

THE ALL IMPORTANT PURCHASE CONTRACT

While conveyancing procedures end with the notary, if there is anything commercially wrong it is too late for alteration. For this reason the **purchase contract** is the most important document in the Spanish buying process. The signing of the contract signifies the following:

- The plan of the house and the location of the plot is satisfactory.
- The *nota simple* has been checked and is in order.
- The contract has been read and understood.
- Signing the contract triggers the release of a normally non-returnable cash deposit.
- The purchaser has the necessary monies, or mortgage, available to complete the transaction.

An English language copy of a contract is reproduced in Appendix 1. It is well written and comprehensive. It is normally set out paragraph by paragraph in Spanish and the mother tongue of the purchaser, thus ensuring no ambiguity. The key points are highlighted below:

- It reconfirms all previous details, namely the parties to the agreement; the ownership of the land, its registration and freedom from debts; details of the plot; the size and description of the property.

- It sets out in detail the payment method, time, currency and amount; financial penalties for failing to complete; emphasises the sale includes the services of water and electricity and the use of the community facilities.

- Confirms that the purchaser respects the obligations of the law surrounding the Community of Owners.

- This particular contract was drawn up by a builder. It is

ambiguous on a firm date for completion and weak on the
penalties for failure to complete on time!

COMMUNITY CHARGES – A SHARE OF THE COSTS

Buying a property in Spain on an urbanisation invariably means
becoming a member of a community of property owners. The
payment of community charges every year entitles the co-owner
to the use of communal facilities, and if so desired the right to
discuss with neighbours at the annual general meeting matters of
common concern.

With a new property on a new urbanisation, the organisation
of the community, the drafting of its rules, electing a president,
appointing an administrator and the fixing of fees, all need to be
settled.

It is advisable to at least understand the approximate
community costs involved prior to signing a contract, but in
most situations this would not materialistically effect the buying
decision. Indeed, with a very new urbanisation an overall budget
will not have been determined.

The allocation of costs will vary. On an urbanisation of 1000
homes of equal size each will carry a charge of 0.1 per cent of
the total expenditure. If, however, the urbanisation had 500 large
and 500 small homes the allocation could be 0.125 and 0.075
per cent respectively. This allocation of costs, called the quota
and expressed as a percentage of total community costs, is
determined at a very early stage in any development. The
information should be available upon signing the contract.

An agenda, minutes of meetings, a list of owners' names with
their allocated quotas and updated payments or debts, are
published for every meeting. The meetings are formal. The
purchase contract, the law surrounding communities and the
local urbanisation rules, bind the purchaser to specific
regulations. Appendix 2 is a good, detailed, example of
community rules.

THE *CERTIFICADO FINAL DE LA DIRECCION DE LA OBRA*

Translated this simply means 'Certificate of the Termination of the Building'. It is a certificate produced by the architect when the house is finally complete. It enables a declaration of a new building to be made at the notary's office and is used to obtain the *Licencia de Primera Ocupacion* detailed below.

THE *LICENCIA DE PRIMERA OCUPACION*

'The Licence of First Occupation' is obtained from the town hall on production of the *Cerificado Final de la Direction de la Obra*. It is a licence to inhabit the property, registers it for the purpose of local taxes and the connection of services.

On new urbanisations, the initial supply of water from external pipes and electricity without metres is obtained from the builder's supply point. The reason for this is simple. The completion and occupation of property is faster than the ability of utility companies to connect their supplies.

A word of warning. The electrical supply company will not connect to an unregistered property.

INSURANCES

The property will probably be insured by the builder during construction and at a low nominal value for twelve months from the date of occupation. A copy of this policy will be available which will state the insured value. When the house is occupied, a top up building policy is all that is required by the new owner. The premium is based on the square metres of the house.

Any additional policy for contents insurance should be dealt with in the normal way.

There is nothing unusual about insurance policies in Spain. While the market leader may be a Spanish company, many

British companies operate in this international market place. A mortgage will be insured by the lender.

THE *ESCRITURA*

The *escritura* is the deed for the property. It is a record of the property at a point in time.

- *Copia simple* (not to be confused with the *nota simple*) is a simple copy of the *escritura*, less the signatures which is sufficient to prove ownership. It is available on the day of signing at the notary and recognised as suitable for most legal purposes. It is normal for the purchaser to hold a copy of this document.

- *Escritura de compraventa* is the document signed in the notary's office.

- *Escritura publica* is the *escritura de compraventa*, complete with many official stamps from the Property Register, converting it into a public document.

The abogado, or the property owner, or in the case of a mortgage the bank manager can hold the *escritura*, but irrespective of who holds it someone has to collect the finished document from the notary. Thousands of *escritura*s lie gathering dust in notaries' offices, uncollected or unregistered because of some minor technicality. In the latter case the property will remain unregistered until the 'problem' has been rectified.

The document itself is written in Spanish legalese, making literal translation almost impossible. The owner never holds the original deed, but the first authorised copy. The original is always held at the notary's office. A second authorised copy can be requested in the event of the first being lost.

No one can doubt the necessity of having a comprehensive document, particularly one which clearly states debts or mortgages, or indeed the transparency of having this document made public. But there is considerable ceremony associated with its preparation and signing which many people believe to be unnecessary.

REGISTRO DE LA PROPIEDAD

This is the last piece of paper in the buying cycle. Strangely it is not the *escritura* that is the final step. The *escritura de compraventa* has to be registered with the Property Register making it an *escritura publica* and being over-stamped *Registro de la propiedad*.

This simple one page document simply closes the loop to the *nota simple* which was considered at the commencement of the buying cycle. What does all this mean? It registers:

- details of the property in a public place
- who has the title
- which notary was responsible for the *escritura*
- details of mortgages.

SMALL BUILDING ALTERATIONS

Although a property has been built to a correct specification, let us assume there is a need to construct a small modification such as a dividing wall between an adjacent property, or perhaps a shed to hold some tools.

Do you need permission to do this? The answer is yes. In fact permission is usually quite straightforward. A visit to the town hall, the completion of a paper entitled *solicitud de licencia de obras*, clearly marked 'minor', and the payment of a small fee, will result in the necessary approval. That is of course provided the modification fits in with the overall urbanisation design, style and specification.

Unfortunately few people do apply. Should one offended neighbour object, or should the alteration infringe community rules, there is a risk of being fined or having to knock the structure down.

CASE STUDY – PURCHASING A PROPERTY WITH A MORTGAGE

Question

We visited Spain about one month ago and decided to buy a house. The agent was most insistent that we sign a contract and pay a deposit of ten per cent as other people were interested in the property. Before we signed the contract we explained to the agent that we required a mortgage in order to complete the purchase. He told us this was 'no problem' and arranged for us to meet a bank manager who informed us that he would be able to lend us 70 per cent of the value of the property. As this was satisfactory for our purposes, we concluded our business and left for home.

Much to our surprise we were informed that the property we were purchasing at 200,000 Euros had been valued at 140,000 Euros and the bank was only prepared to loan us 98,000 Euros (70 per cent of 140,000) compared to our expectation of 140,000 Euros (70 per cent of 200,000).

We now cannot afford to complete the purchase. Our question is 'what can we do?'

Answer

In order for the bank to issue a mortgage loan, they have to have the property valued and for this purpose they use a valuation company. It is normal for a valuation company to undervalue using a 'worst case scenario' instead of the current market value. It is unlikely that the bank will increase their percentage offer and equally unlikely the valuation company will alter their assessment.

It is very important to obtain professional advice before signing any document and parting with any money. It is true

---

that sometimes another person is interested in the same property, but this ploy is often used by agents to quickly get a signature on a contract. Obviously the best course of action would have been to sign nothing until the mortgage situation was clear.

What is the position now? This can only be answered by reference to the contract. If the contract states that the deposit will be forfeited in the event of non completion, then unfortunately that is the situation unless an amicable arrangement can be agreed with the agent and vendor.

It would have been possible to have a non-standard clause in the contract stating that a mortgage loan is required in order to complete the purchase, and in the event of this amount of finance not being forthcoming, the agent or vendor is obliged to give a full refund of the deposit. This situation is too late for that.

Obviously the matter can be discussed with the agent and vendor but it is definitely a 'sticky wicket'. A compromise solution with a refund of half the deposit, giving some compensation to the vendors, would seem a good idea.

SUMMARY

- There are 11 steps in the standard purchasing and conveyancing procedure for a new property.

- Additional steps would be a mortgage, and gaining planning permission for a small alteration.

- All documents are important. There are four key documents but the most important is the contract.

- The *escritura*, too is an official document of great importance. It legalises the sale and purchase. Commercially it records what has been agreed previously.

7

Money Matters

PROPERTY PRICES

Property prices will vary according to supply and demand, their
location, size and position. It is therefore not possible to give an
authoritative price guide for all Spanish property which is best
obtained by referring to property magazines or English language
newspapers. As a guide, however, there is a 125 kilometre strip
of coastline between Alicante and Cartagena which is
developing at a prodigious rate. These properties are heavily
advertised in the European press with the following price
indicators:

* 2 bedroom apartment   80,000 Euros
* 3 bedroom corner duplex   145,000 Euros
* 3 bedroom detached villa   200,000 Euros
* Individually designed 3 bedroom villa   from 250,000 Euros

Using these benchmark property prices it is possible to make
some additional generalised statements.

* Property is more expensive adjacent to the coast and cheaper
  15 kilometres inland.

* Property is more expensive on the Costa del Sol, the Canary
  and Balearic Islands

* Property is generally cheaper the further you travel north.

* Property in Andalusia, the home of white walled individual

properties restored or in need of renovation, can be surprisingly expensive if only a short distance from the Costa del Sol.

- Within each region it is possible to find exclusive areas of new property attracting prices of 400,000 Euros and, conversely, close by in working towns cheaper property renovated to a high standard at around 100,000 Euros.

A NATIONAL PICTURE

The latest national figures for property prices per square metre are now:

Price per square meter Madrid – the most expensive	2075 Euros
Price per square meter Costa Blanca – the cheapest Mediterranean homes	1780 Euros
Price per square meter Huesca – the lowest priced region	820 Euros

PAYING THE MONEY

New property
> 10 per cent on signing the contract
> 40 per cent stage payment
> 25 per cent stage payment
> 25 per cent on completion

Resale property
> 10 per cent on signing the contract
> 90 per cent on completion

A partly built property
> 50 per cent on signing the contract (walls, roof, windows and doors completed)
> 25 per cent stage payment
> 25 per cent on completion

The basic rules

- A deposit of ten per cent or less is normal for a new or resale property. For a partly built property it will vary according to the amount of work completed. It is payable by cash or banker's draft to the agent or to the seller.

- All payments can be negotiated.

- The deposit is non returnable if the buyer fails to complete unless there is a clause in the contract to the contrary.

- If the builder fails to deliver a new property on time penalty charges accrue. Again these should be stated in the contract. In practice the contract will always state a flexible date of completion.

- If a seller fails to complete the transaction the buyer is recompensed to a value twice the amount of the deposit unless the contract states otherwise.

- Final and stage payments should be paid by banker's draft in Euros.

ALLOWING FOR ADDITIONAL BUYING COSTS

It is normal to allow ten per cent of the property value declared in the *escritura* for the additional costs in buying which cover three taxes, two fees and charges from the *abogado*. A breakdown of these costs are as follows:

- Transfer tax or IVA (value added tax) 7 per cent
- Stamp duty (on a new property only) 0.5 per cent
- Plus valia tax 0.5 per cent
- Notary fees 0.5 per cent
- Property register fees 0.5 per cent
- Charges from the *abogado* 1.0 per cent

Transfer tax and IVA

Impuesto de Transmisiones Patrimoniales is the Spanish for transfer tax which is charged on a sale between two individuals. IVA, the Spanish equivalent of Value Added Tax, is a business charge on a sale between say, a property company and an individual. Governments can vary taxes, and they do, but it is normal to allow seven per cent for either of these two taxes.

Stamp duty

Stamp duty of 0.5 per cent is payable on a new property. It is not payable on a resale property.

Plus valia tax

Plus valia is payable on a resale property and a new property. It is assessed locally on the increase in the value of the land since the previous owner bought the property or a developer bought the land. An apartment on an urbanisation where little land is involved or where there has been no increase in value in a short time will suffer a low plus valia tax charge. Conversely a home with a large plot of land, held by the previous owner for say, 30 years, will suffer a high charge.

Of course it is the seller who should pay this tax. He has gained the benefit of the increase in land value. The law of the country supports this view. In practice, however, this tax has often fallen on the purchaser since it a more secure method of collection by the town hall. After all, a vendor may flee the country leaving this tax unpaid.

A purchaser may feel, quite rightly, aggrieved at paying this tax. The recourse is simply to have a clause inserted in the contract stating it is the vendor who pays the plus valia tax and withholding this sum from the final payment.

Notary fees

These vary according to the value of the property declared in the *escritura* and the number of pages in the document. Allow 350 Euros or 0.5 per cent.

Property registry

Again there is a fee to have the property registered. It is wise to allow a similar figure of 0.5 per cent.

Charges from the *abogado*

Naturally this fee will depend on the amount of work done. If the basic paperwork has been handled to a straightforward conclusion then the charge will be low. If on the other hand there have been complications or the need to draw up multi-lingual contracts then the charges will be higher. Allow one per cent for this charge.

Who pays?

The buyer and seller can agree between themselves who pays these taxes, fees and charges. This can be incorporated into the contract and is not overridden by Spanish law. In practice, however, the buyer pays either directly, or on occasions indirectly when the agent incorporates these charges into an overall selling price. *Todos los gastos* is the Spanish phrase meaning 'all expenses arising'.

It is also normal practice to deposit the approximate figure of ten per cent of the *escritura* value with the *abogado* or the bank manager (for mortgaged properties), who will pay these accounts on behalf of the buyer, submitting an itemised statement when the transactions are completed.

Five per cent tax deposit

One last twist in the tail. If a property is bought from a non-resident, which is unlikely with a new property but quite possible with a resale property, then 5 per cent of the purchase price declared on the *escritura* must be deposited with the tax office in the vendor's name. In other words only 95 per cent is paid directly to the vendor.

Why? This deposit is designed to cover the non-resident's liability for taxes, and in the main, capital gains tax.

THE BLACK ECONOMY AND BLACK MONEY

It is quite common in Spain to have two purchase prices for a property:

- One price is the actual price paid exclusive of any fees or taxes.

- The other is a lower price declared in the *escritura*.

- As a guideline, the difference between the two prices should be less than 15 to 20 per cent.

- The difference between the two prices is normally paid to the vendor in cash.

This practice is known to agents, buyers and sellers, builders and developers, the *abogado*, the bank manager and the notary. It is known by the tax authorities. In fact it is known by everyone.

It is a mechanism of tax evasion which if not radically abused, is tolerated by the Spanish tax man. All taxes and fees are calculated on the value stated in the *escritura*, not the actual price paid. The transfer tax or IVA charged at seven per cent is effectually reduced to 5.6 per cent if the *escritura* value is declared at 80 per cent of the actual sum paid. When re-selling the same property at a later date a similar reduction needs to be applied to avoid the excessive payment of capital gains as this too is based on the value declared in the *escritura*.

Many people are now seeing the folly of this practice but once started it is difficult to stop. The saving of say, 1.4 per cent in initial taxes when purchasing can easily be outweighed by a greater loss in capital gains when re-selling.

Spanish tax men do not sit idly by. Renowned for being sharp but pragmatic, they maintain their own table of property values and are empowered to set a higher value on the sale which can result in an additional tax bill should they feel excessive tax avoidance has taken place. This scrutiny is mainly applied, but not exclusively, to the purchaser's tax liability.

'Black' is the term used to describe the difference between the actual price paid and the value declared in the *escritura*. 'Black money' describes the cash payment representing the difference in values. 'Black economy', however, has a far wider meaning, both in Spain and in other European countries, being the 'cash for services' market designed to avoid the payment of value added tax.

MORE CAPITAL COSTS?

Resale homes normally come fully furnished, especially when the owners are returning to their homeland. But it may be necessary to purchase additional items for a new home. They could be:

- kitchen appliances, light fittings, bathroom fittings
- furniture, bedding, curtains
- security grilles or burglar alarms
- patio, driveway and shrubs for the garden
- connection charges for telephone, water, and electricity
- a car or other means of transport.

WHAT ARE THE ANNUAL RUNNING COSTS OF A SPANISH HOME?

Running costs will of course vary according to the size of the property. But as a guide, a retired couple, living all year round in a three bedroom house on an urbanisation, with no central heating, could expect bills similar to the following:

Telephone	1,000 Euros
Electricity	500 Euros
Gas	200 Euros
Water	500 Euros
House/property insurance	150 Euros
Local taxes	500 Euros
Community charges	150 Euros
Total	3,000 Euros per year

This low domestic bill is of course a reflection of living in a warm climate with low energy needs. But there are other items of expenditure, not strictly related to maintaining a home, such as medical insurance, and motoring costs which also need to be taken into account.

Medical insurance	800 Euros per person per year dependent on age
Motoring costs	5,000 Euros per year covering fuel, insurance and depreciation, all of which can obviously vary.

- Telefonica, the Spanish telephone company, is a major communication organisation within the European market place. It has a good reputation for service and efficiency with consumer prices similar to other European countries.

- Iberdrola, the Spanish electricity supply company, is not quite so reliable. It is not unusual to have disruptions to supply and service can be slow. The high unit prices are decreasing each year.

- Gas supply is by bottles, or on large urbanisations from a central supply point. The service is good but, due to the door to door distribution system, very labour intensive.

- There is more water consumed per head of population in Spain than in any other European country. This is a remarkable statistic. However, most of this is used in agriculture, leaving drinking water in some coastal areas both scarce and impure. Very little water is wasted. Desalination plants are commonplace as the political masters of towns and cities seek to increase water supply.

- Insurance charges across Europe are similar.

- Local taxes and community charges are low. This service will always attract its critics but it is exceptionally good value for money.

SUMMARY

- Property prices can vary from 80,000 Euros to 450,000 Euros depending on size, location and position.

- Additional buying costs are around ten per cent which covers taxes, fees and legal costs. The buyer normally pays.

- There are often two purchase prices for a property. One is the actual price paid. The other is the price declared in the *escritura*. Tax avoidance at purchase is a short term economy as capital gains tax has to be considered when re-selling.

- With a new property, additional costs will arise fitting out kitchens and bathrooms, installing lights, ensuring security, and laying out a garden. A resale property often comes with all fittings, furniture and the garden established.

- To give a benchmark, the annual running cost of a home is about 3,000 Euros.

8

Before You Go

LEARNING THE LANGUAGE

Spanish business people can generally speak English and German in addition to their native tongue. Waiters and shop assistants too can often manage a few English words. Builders, repair men, installation engineers, petrol attendants, postmen, policemen and hospital staff generally only speak Spanish.

It is just about possible to live in Spain without speaking Spanish. Interpreters or friends can be used as an aid to discussion. The use of body language, pointing, nodding and shrugging can also assist. Enhancement of communication with a few key words such as *si, una, por favor, gracias* (not necessarily in that order) is a step in the right direction. But the non-linguist needs one other major phrase '*Hable Ingles, por favor*?' (Can you speak English, please?).

There can be no substitute for learning the basics of the Spanish language. After all, it is their country we are choosing to visit or live in. We can surely be polite and respectful by learning a few words. Spanish people appreciate those who try and politely smile when they get it wrong.

How do you learn the language?

Home study courses by book and audiotape are heavily advertised. They are an excellent, intensive, medium for learning at a time best suited to the individual.

Many intensive language schools operate in Spain with prospectuses aimed at a variety of levels in many European languages.

One of the best learning methods by far, before leaving home, is an old fashioned adult evening class at a local school or college. A bit of fun, a common purpose, which together with some effort for 20 to 25 evenings, will get the average person to a decent basic linguistic standard.

CASE STUDY – A TYPICAL LANGUAGE LESSON

Picture a typical class. Fifteen adults squeezing their posteriors onto seats designed for 12-year-olds. The walls of the room are covered by algebraic equations long since forgotten. Friendly but nervous conversation falls silent as the 7.00 pm starting time approaches.

The door opens. '*Hola, como te llamas*?' is spoken by a five feet tall, 40-year-old lady with black wiry hair, wearing dark clothes covered with a small floral print. Her skin is olive and her eyes gleam like that of an animal's caught in the headlights of a car. She moves quickly to the centre of the room, turns to the class and again repeats the phrase: '*Hola, como te llamas*?' (What is your name?)

The phrase is repeated not once, but many times. It is written on the blackboard. It is repeated many times by the anxious students. Much to everyone's surprise replies are forthcoming:

'*Hola, me llamo*, Heather.'

'*Me llamo*, Peter.'

'Mary.'

The class progresses with repetition being the order of the day. Not a word of English is spoken. In fact the learning process decrees that speaking English is forbidden. The welcome coffee break is extended from ten to 20 minutes with one nervous class member saying, 'I knew the answer until she pointed at me, then my mind went blank.'

The evening proceedes at a fast and furious pace.

Q '*De donde eres*?' (Where are you from?)

A '*Soy de Edinburgh, y vivo en London*' (I am from Edinburgh, I live in London).

Q '*Hablas Ingles*?' (Do you speak English?)

A '*Si, hablo Ingles y un poco de Espanol*' (Yes, I speak

English and a little bit of Spanish).

The first evening, returning to school for the first time in 30 to 40 years, is not easy for any adult. The exhausted but enthusiastic students go home to complete, with a great deal of effort, the set homework.

uno, dos, tres, cuatro, cinco, seis, siete, ocho, nueve, diez
hijo, hija, hermano, hermana, padre, madre
pintora, cocinera, carpintero, medico, estudiante

Fortunately future lessons get easier as key words and phrases are assimilated. The 'food and drink' lesson is learnt with ease.

'*Dos cafés con leche, una tapa de jamon y una tapa de queso, por favor*' (two coffees with milk, one *tapa* of ham, one *tapa* of cheese, please).

Learning packages generally follow BBC publications entitled *Viva Espana* or *Suenos*. Adults need all the help they can get to assimilate a new language and this is supplied by a combination of book, audiotape, class work, TV or video.

TAKING YOUR PETS

There is absolutely no reason why a pet cannot be taken to Spain, or for that matter travel through an intermediate country such as France. The United Kingdom has recently relaxed their views on quarantine regulations, bringing their approach more in line with other European countries. It may be necessary to travel to and from Spain frequently or unexpectedly, in which case any pet should have the necessary vaccinations, health checks and accompanying paperwork.

Spain has the normal catteries and kennels. It has many fully qualified veterinary surgeons. Urbanisations, towns and cities have codes of behaviour for dogs which results in them being banned from beaches and other public places.

Cruelty

There is another side to keeping a pet in Spain: the heartless attitude of some Spanish people to animals and in particular to dogs, which are often tied up all day, or left to roam the streets, or even simply abandoned. Keeping a large dog is often seen as a necessity for guarding a home, but the ability to bark is not a guarantee of home security.

The Spanish are not a nation of animal lovers. There are dog refuge organisations in most coastal towns, invariably run by resident British or Germans who often witness many barbaric acts committed on these defenceless animals.

LETTING THE HOUSE BACK HOME

Some people, having purchased a Spanish home with the intention of living there permanently, are reluctant to immediately sell their old home. No matter the care or planning that has gone into the selection of a new home in the sun, it may not work out. Retaining a base back home lessens this risk, offering a bolthole in the event of any change in circumstance.

There are two major reasons for letting out a property:

- income
- security – an empty property is potentially at risk during the dark winter months.

Letting companies

It makes sense to put the letting of a property in the hands of experts. The Association of Residential Agents, formed in 1981, regulates letting agents and seeks to promote the provision of high standards of service to both landlords and tenants. Membership is restricted to those letting agents who can demonstrate good financial practices and whose staff have a good working knowledge of all the legal issues involved.

A choice of letting services

There are three main types of letting service:

- letting only

- letting and rent collection
- letting and full management.

Cost and risk should determine the service selected. The greater the service, the greater the letting cost. The greater the cost the less risk of unsavoury tenants or damage to the property and its fittings.

Taxation

If the owner is classed as an overseas resident for tax purposes, the letting company is responsible for deducting income tax at base rate on the rental income, unless the Inland Revenue provides a tax exemption certificate.

Charges

A letting company will charge around 15 per cent of the rental income for a full service together with charges for introducing tenants and drawing up agreements. Taxation and letting charges can therefore reduce gross letting income by 30 to 40 per cent.

MOVING YOUR FURNITURE

Spanish furniture is attractive, distinctive and ornate, but is not to everyone's taste. Moving comfortable furniture from home, bits and pieces that one has grown accustomed to, is often preferred.

European removal companies are sound professional organisations normally belonging to the International Federation of Furniture Removers. They have well-established procedures both operationally and administratively. The packing and paperwork are best left to them. While it is obvious that more than one competitive quote is necessary, the cheapest company should be one who offers a shared service with depots close to both the old home and the new Spanish home. The cost of moving an average home, including insurance, calculated according to the number of cubic metres required is around 3,500 to 5,000 Euros. Cost reduction is best achieved by flexibility in pick-up and delivery dates. Transit time is approximately two weeks.

It is wise to leave TV sets at home as the Spanish sound system and the receiving frequency differs from other European countries. Washing machines work successfully but the plumbing of a Spanish home does not allow for a hot water fill. Computers, vacuum cleaners and other domestic items all operate successfully on Spanish voltages.

ORGANISING YOUR TRAVEL

Flights

There are daily scheduled flights to Spain by the recognised major national carriers and the Spanish carrier Iberia. Standard fares are charged.

However, the cheapest and most frequently used method of air travel is a last minute booking, on a charter flight or low cost carrier at around 100 Euros one way. Tickets are best obtained from a flight only shop, direct from a low cost carrier, or through the many internet sites devoted to low cost travel.

Alicante, Malaga, Majorca and Tenerife are the most frequently used Spanish airports. Within Spain a daily shuttle service operates between Madrid and its regional capitals.

Data from the Association of European Airlines shows that 24 per cent of European flights were delayed by more than 15 minutes. Madrid is the worst with 36 per cent of departures delayed for on average 43 minutes and Gatwick is one of the best with only 19 per cent of flights delayed. Heathrow is the worst UK airport.

Car hire

It makes sense to pre-book car hire at the same time as booking air tickets. It avoids delay on arrival, as the car should be ready.

All the international car hire companies operate in Spain together with many Spanish national and regional operators. It is a fiercely competitive market. *Coche de alquiuer* (car hire) can also be booked at airports or in large towns.

E-COMMERCE

Travel is the fastest growing area of e-commerce. The web and travel go very well together. It is a service. There is nothing to deliver other than the confirmation of a booking. Information can be updated very quickly online, making it perfect for accessing the latest deals.

A new resident of Spain will not greatly benefit from this development unless travelling back home regularly. It will, however, benefit someone who has bought a holiday home for use three or four times per year. Booking flights or ferries, arranging car rental and currency are achieved by a few mouse-clicks.

SUMMARY

- It is better to learn the basics of the Spanish language. It makes day to day communication easier. It also demonstrates respect to the inhabitants of the country.

- By all means take your pet but remember Spain is not renowned for its love of animals.

- Moving permanently to Spain for the first time is a risk which can be lessened by letting out your property back home. It is best to let the property through a professionally recognised agent.

- Many furniture removal companies have depots in Spain.

- Travel is best achieved through buying tickets from flight only shops, low-cost airlines or through ever increasing internet booking services.

9

Linking It All Together

MOVING IN

The new property is ready. After a long wait and some inevitable building delays notification has been received from the agent that 'the property can now be occupied'. There is a lot of work to be done. Moving house at the best of times is stressful, moving to Spain – either to a holiday home or permanent one – conjures up emotions of excitement and hard work.

In practical terms there is a need to carry out a series of tasks in a focused, planned and methodical way. The majority of agents offer some assistance at this difficult moving-in stage. This can be very helpful. The first few days in a foreign country, making a number of decisions with differing customs and procedures, can be disconcerting. A knowledgeable hand is very welcome at speeding up the process by going to the correct place, in the correct sequence, at the correct time.

- If need be, organise furniture removal from home, book air tickets, hotel and car rental.

- Look at the new house to ensure there are no faults.

- Visit the *abogado* to ask him to arrange an appointment with the notary for the signing of the *escritura* and for the final payment to the builder.

- Visit the bank to collect a banker's draft for the final payment on the house (plus the inevitable black money) and another draft for payment to the *abogado*.

- Complete the payment and signing procedures at the notary. Obtain the keys and a *copia simple*.

- If required purchase kitchen equipment, bathroom fittings, lights and furniture.

VIEWING THE NEW PROPERTY FOR THE FIRST TIME

Having seen a show house, some brochures, a plan and location diagram, the viewing of your own completely new house for the first time is approached with considerable enthusiasm and excitement.

'It is there where it should be. The white walls with ochre coloured window frames are set against a clear blue sky. Inside the walls too are white, contrasting with the dark orange bathroom tiles. A bidet too! The bedrooms are large, spacious with fitted wardrobes. Yes, it's exactly what we specified.'

On the down side the roads may not be finished, the water and electric still to be supplied by the builder through pipes and cables, the garden non-existent and the house probably needs a good clean.

The emotion and pleasure of seeing a new home for the first time needs to be quickly replaced with a more logical approach. In a new home, even with a ten-year guarantee, some faults are inevitable. At this point inspect the property thoroughly, recording all faults.

Major faults

If any major faults exist, immediately stop the purchasing process until they are rectified. Go back home if need be, but on no account make the final payment. This of course is an unlikely scenario, after all the building has been inspected by the architect. But to be realistic major faults can and do happen.

Time for talking it may be, but time for action is more important and this is best achieved on the part of the purchaser by refusing to make the final payment.

Minor faults

Draw up a list of minor faults (known as a snagging list) and give it to the builder. Rectifying building faults at the best of times is a wearisome process and in Spain it is no better. Delays, procrastination and battling with the attitude of *mañana* will result in considerable frustration. But remember it is Spain, where time is not important, so constant friendly pressure will be necessary to sort out all these faults.

REVISITING THE *ABOGADO*

It is now time to revisit the *abogado*. He will have been seen before when taking legal advice. He will now require a payment to complete the conveyancing of the property, which we know to be about ten per cent with hopefully a small refund at a later date. At this hectic stage in proceedings it is important for the purchaser not to get bogged down in legal mumbo-jumbo. Just let the *abogado* get on with it. Understand the principles, which are essentially:

- Making arrangements with the purchaser, the seller and the notary for the preparation and signing of the *escritura*.

- Making arrangements with the builder for the final payment.

- Making payments on behalf of the purchaser for conveyancing costs and taxes.

- When at the notary's office, ensuring the purchaser fully understands a verbal translation of the *escritura* from the Spanish language into his native tongue.

- Ensuring the entire conveyancing procedure is carried out correctly.

- If the purchaser(s) cannot be present at the signing of the *escritura* final arrangements must be made to grant a power of attorney to the *abogado* or to an other named person (see Chapter 5).

- Applying for *Numero de Identification de Extranjero* (NIE).

Fiscal identification number

All residents or non-residents with financial dealings in Spain must have an identification number. This is called the *Numero de Identification de Extranjero*. It is popularly called an NIE for short, the significant word *extranjero* meaning foreigner. NIF, or *Numero de Identification Fiscal*, is the fiscal number which is the same as the NIE number. This serves as a Fiscal, Identity, and in the case of Spaniards a Passport Number.

It is easy to get an NIE. A visit to the foreigners department of a police station will suffice. A passport with a copy, two photographs and completion of the relevant form is all that is required. But long queues can be avoided by asking the *abogado* to complete this task since it is an essential document for the registration of the *escritura*.

Non-residents will quickly become accustomed to a way of life dependent on personal identification by a passport or NIE number. Residents will also have a *residencia* number to contend with. In addition to purchasing a property the NIE is required for:

- the purchase of a car and other expensive items
- dealing with the tax authorities
- identification on other documents such as insurance policies or bank records.

Future relationships

Like any good businessman, the *abogado* will seek to retain a future relationship with his clients after the conveyancing has been completed. There are taxes to be dealt with. Wills to be prepared. New permanent residents have even greater bureaucracy to deal with, involving an application for *residencia*, driving licence transfer and possible entry into the medical system.

It certainly is convenient to have a one-stop-shop for all administrative, legal and fiscal affairs. But of course, as we have said before, a *gestor* can do most of this.

REVISITING THE BANK

The previous visit to the bank was of course to open an account. In the intervening period regular sums of money should have been transferred to cover:

- the final payment to the builder
- the costs of conveyancing and taxes
- anticipated payments for fittings, furniture, and the garden
- the possible purchase of a car
- a contingency sum.

This is a substantial amount; the first two items alone totalling 35 per cent of the purchase price. Twenty-five per cent will be the final property payment and of course ten per cent for the conveyancing costs including taxes. To avoid any currency fluctuation it would have been wise to have transferred this money in small regular amounts over a period of time but conversely, money sitting in a Spanish bank account attracts little interest.

Should 'black money' be involved, part of the final payment will be in cash. While banks are well accustomed to paying out large quantities of cash, advance notification is necessary to ensure these amounts are available.

CASE STUDY – DON'T GET MUGGED

New owner: I expect there will be long queues at the bank. *Firma* here, *firma* there, that sort of thing.

Agent: Probably Senor, probably. Are you aware that seven per cent of the total payment is cash for the builder?

New owner: No.

Agent: You are now!

New owner: Let me understand this. This house cost 100,000 Euros. Today's final payment of 25 per cent is 25,000 Euros of which 7,000 Euros are cash and 18,000 Euros are a banker's draft.

Agent: Yes, that's how things are done here. By the way the house costs 93,000 Euros. Do you understand? This will benefit you too. Less tax to pay.
(He taps his nose twice with the index finger of the right hand.)

New owner: Presumably this transaction is known to the appropriate authorities?

Agent: Si, Senor, everyone knows.
(The money is collected and placed in a black briefcase.)

Agent: Let us go Senor, to pay the builder at the notary's office. We do not want to get mugged!

THE FINAL PAYMENT

The final payment to the seller, in this case the builder, or his representative at the notary's office, is not the most complicated of procedures, but two extremely important points arise. They are for the protection of the buyer.

• Ensure a receipt is given which also covers any 'black money' payment.

- Ensure the receipt states the 'property is paid in full'.

GOING TO THE NOTARY

The meeting at the notary's office to agree and sign the *escritura* can last about two hours. Just about everyone involved with the sale and purchase attends. The notary's office can on occasions get very crowded with many transactions taking place simultaneously.

In some busy offices, dealing with a conveyor belt of new properties, the task is concluded simply with the builder's clerk (the seller), the buyer, the *abogado*'s assistant who is also the translator and the notary himself. A maximum of four people.

But it is not always like this. With a resale property, an agent, a solicitor, a bank manager to give a mortgage and another to redeem a mortgage, two sellers and two buyers, the notary and his assistant can bring the total to ten people. Hopefully, someone can be the translator.

The buyer's objectives are clear

- To make the final payment to the seller, which may include some black money.

- If a mortgage is involved, ensure this payment is made directly by the lender to the seller.

- Ensure the *escritura* is signed to the satisfaction of both the notary and the *abogado*.

- Take time to understand the contents of the *escritura*.

- Receive the keys to the property.

- Obtain a *copia simple*.

EQUIPPING THE HOME

As an alternative to moving furniture from home, all items can be purchased in Spain. Furniture packages to equip an entire home are readily available. They come in different sizes, style and quality. The range can cover a simple two-bedroom holiday home to a large expensive package, in a distinctive, colourful, Spanish style, for a permanent home.

'Price and service' is the key while purchasing these packages. Is the supplier recommended? Are the goods in stock? Can they be delivered in a few days? It is easy to give and take an order, but with so many items in the package it is important to have a guaranteed delivery time for them all.

SUMMARY

- Moving into a new Spanish home can be stressful but exciting. An offer of help by the agent should be welcomed.

- Always inspect a new property for faults before proceeding to the final stages of payment.

- By all means let the *abogado* carry out the conveyancing but be wary of a long term business relationship as the gestor offers an alternative for dealing with fiscal matters.

- Making the final payment to the builder may involve 'black money'. Ensure the receipt is fully understood, free from ambiguity and states the total price has been paid.

- Going to the notary is the keystone to the conveyancing procedure. Keep the objectives clear. Do not get overwhelmed by the formality of the occasion.

- 'Price and service' is the key when purchasing furniture packages.

10

Buying Other Properties

The standard procedure to be followed when purchasing a new house was outlined in Chapter 6. Let us now look at some other types of property purchase and their conveyancing procedures (see Figure 12).

The previous advice given still applies, namely all documentary steps are important and failure to complete one may have serious consequences but the most important documents are the *nota simple*, the contract, the community rules and the *escritura*. Of these the contract is the most important.

FAST TRACK CONVEYANCING FOR NEW HOUSES

In some areas of Spain and especially around Torrevieja, the whole regional infrastructure is devoted to the marketing of property yet to be constructed.

In addition to house building, indigenous industries such as furniture making have sprung up. Service industries too, such as car hire, hotels, banking and restaurants, have expanded to meet the demand of people buying homes for holiday or for permanent residence.

In this area all the procedures involving the purchase of new properties have been simplified and speeded-up. Fast track conveyancing is quite different from the standard procedure and is modified to recognise the following:

- The property is purchased from building plans probably following an inspection flight or a short stay in the area.

Check boundaries
Check water rights
Check road access over the land
Check utility supplies
Check for other building development
Check planning permission
Obtain copy of the seller's *escritura*
Obtain copy of the seller's passport or *residencia*
Obtain copy of the seller's *certificado de empadronamiento*
If furnished, obtain a copy of the furniture inventory
Obtain copy of bills for utilities, rates, community
Obtain a plan of the house
Obtain a drawing locating the plot
Obtain the *nota simple*
Obtain details of the community charges
Sign the agent's agreement
Sign the contract, pay the deposit
Obtain *Certificado Final de la Direccion de la Obra*
Obtain the *Licencia de Primera Ocupacion*
Final payment to builder, obtain keys
Arrange insurances
Sign the *escritura*, obtain *copia simple*
Final payment, sign *escritura*, obtain *copia simple*
Change services and utilities into new names
Collect *escritura* and *Registro de la Propiedad*
Obtain building permit – *Permiso de Obra*
Appoint architect and builder if required
Renovate and / or build. New *escritura* required

Code
NP/SP New property/Standard procedure
NP/FT New property/Fast track procedure
RS – Resale   FR – For renovation   BYO – Build Your Own

Fig. 12. Different purchasing procedures

NP/SP	NP/FT	RS	FR	BYO
				√
				√
				√
				√
			√	√
			√	√
		√	√	√
		√	√	√
		√		
		√		
		√		
√	√	√		
√	√			
√	√	√	√	√
√	√	√		
√	√			
√	√	√	√	√
√	√			
√	√			
	√			
√	√	√		
	√			
√		√	√	√
		√		
√	√	√	√	√
			√	√
			√	√
			√	√
			√	√

- There will be a 12 to 18 month wait for the property to be completed.

- When notified that the property has been completed, the purchaser naturally wishes to move in immediately. Time is important. No one wants to be held up waiting for legal matters to be completed.

- Making the final payment to the builder, moving in immediately, and letting the legal people 'sort out' the paperwork (the *escritura*) is the core of the fast track approach.

The 12 step fast track procedure

1. A plan of the house
2. Locating the plot
3. The agent's agreement
4. The *nota simple*
5. The contract
6. Community charges – a share of the costs
7. The *Certificado Final de la Direccion de la Obra*
8. The *Licencia de Primera Ocupacion*
9. Paying in full and receiving the keys
10. Insurances
11. The *escritura*
12. *Registro de la Propiedad*

In comparison with the standard conveyancing procedure, a further step is introduced, namely paying the builder, receiving the keys and then going to the notary within 14 days to sign the *escritura*. To emphasise this point – the final payment is separate from the legal proceedings at the notary's office. It is this payment, correctly recorded, which is the core of the fast track conveyancing procedure ensuring the purchaser gains access to the property immediately without waiting for the *escritura* to be prepared by the notary.

The contract in Appendix 1 makes reference to this arrangement in clause Six.

CASE STUDY – PAYING THE BUILDER

It is now time to take possession of the property. The architect says the building is complete. The town hall says the property can be inhabited. The agent says everything is in order. The purchaser wishes to occupy the property immediately. The builder wants his money.

So to the builder, with a banker's order and a bundle of notes. The builder's clerk is a young woman who wears the standard black, tight, flared trousers associated with smart business attire. She smiles in a tired sort of way, exhibiting years of experience as she carefully counts the money.

As the task is completed she smiles again and says, '*No para mi*' (not for me). A key is pressed on a word processor and a document is produced which when translated states the full price for the house has been paid. Ambiguity par excellence.

The property....................................has been fully paid, including electric and water installation, by a banker's draft from...Bank and a cash payment both totalling....................................Euros. Any extras, the client promises to pay on the day of signing the *escritura*. This document entitles the client to receive the keys to the property.

Signed..(builder)

She smiles for the third time and in a kindly way says, 'Here are your keys and receipt. *Bien suerte* (good luck)'.

RESALE HOUSES

As a resale house has been lived-in for some time, several of the steps necessary for buying a new property can be discarded. But new steps take their place. Let's look at this.

1. Obtain a copy of the seller's *escritura*.

2. Obtain a copy of the *nota simple*.
3. Obtain a copy of the seller's passport or *residencia*.
4. Obtain a copy of the seller's *certificado de empadronamiento* which will have been issued by the town hall and simply states the names of those residing at the address.
5. Although not always possible, try to obtain a copy of a scale drawing of the property.
6. If sold furnished, obtain a signed copy of the furniture inventory.
7. Obtain the last copy of the paid bills for utilities such as water, electric, and telephone, together with rates and community charges. The administrator of the community will issue a certificate stating the date to which the community charges have been paid.
8. Sign the contract and pay the deposit.
9. Sign the *escritura*. Make the final payment. Obtain the *copia simple*.
10. Arrange insurances.
11. Ensure service and utility supply accounts are changed into the new owner's name.
12. Obtain a final copy of the *escritura* and the *Registro de la Propiedad*.

- Steps 1 to 4 inclusive simply ensure that the person who is selling the house has the right to do so. The name(s) on all the documents should be the same. If not it is important to find out why. The agent selling the property should have checked this out but it does no harm to check personally.

- The dimensions of the property in the *escritura* should agree with the dimensions in a scale drawing. If not, this requires investigating as building alterations may have taken place.

- The seller's *escritura*, the *nota simple* and the checks in step 7 will give details of mortgages and encumbrances on the

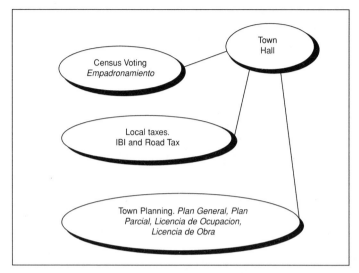

Fig. 13. The importance of the town hall.

property which have to be addressed in the conveyancing procedure.

- The *copia simple* is the necessary identification required by utility suppliers in order to change the name and payment details.

RENOVATED OR REFORMED HOUSES

Whatever the state of repair of a building, the renovated or reformed house conveyancing procedure starts with the purchase of a property. It may be run down. It may even be a ruin. It is probably in the country but can equally be an old home in a Spanish town. Either way, the starting point is the purchase of a resale house.

Since the external structure of the building will probably be altered, a number of checks need to be carried out before purchasing.

- Check with the planning department at the town hall exactly what can be done: demolish and rebuild, extend or simply renovate are the obvious options.

- With a town house, renovation and an upward extension are probably the only possibilities.

- In the country do not assume anything is possible. In fact the height, size and the number of properties per 1,000 or 10,000 square metres is regulated by the town hall planning department.

- Check the utility supplies. If there are none how much will it cost to install them? Important questions need to be answered about the supply of electric, water and communication systems.

- Assuming these checks are satisfactory it is now safe to purchase the property.

- Obtain a building permit, called *Permiso de Obra* (permission to build) from the town hall which may cost up to four per cent of the estimated material cost of construction.

- Lastly, when building work is complete, don't forget the *Certificado Final de la Direccion de la Obra* and the *Licencia de Primera Ocupacion.*

- The description of the property in the *escritura* should be updated in line with the new building structure, and a *copia simple* obtained.

- Obtain a final copy of the *escritura* and the Registro de la Propiedad.

BUILDING YOUR OWN HOME

Building your own home is an extension of the principles outlined above under 'renovated or reformed houses'. The first addition is obviously the purchase of the land itself and the second is the appointment of an architect and builder. But to some people the challenge and charm is to treat it as a DIY project.

It has been stated before that legal advice should always be taken when purchasing in Spain. Nowhere is this advice more necessary than when dealing with the complexities of land purchase, particularly rural land. Equally the drawing up of an agreement with an architect and builder will benefit from some common sense knowledge and legal advice.

- Does the seller have the right to sell the land?

- Are the boundaries clearly marked? They are normally marked by stakes, or painted and numbered on the rocks.

- Where crops and trees are growing, or the land may be used for agricultural purposes, check the water rights.

- Check the road access, particularly for winter rain. Are there any roads, or is there a right of way across the land?

- Are there any building developments, or roads planned close by? Will the property be overlooked by any other higher development obstructing the line of sight?

- Once the land has been acquired will building permission be granted? What size and type of building will be allowed by the planning authorities?

- Remember the purchase of the land necessitates an *escritura*. The building of a property a second *escritura*. Further extensions can involve a third.

- The appointment of an architect and builder has to be considered.

- What are the architect's fees and how are they paid?

- A plan and building specification is drawn up by the architect.

- The contractual agreement with the builder is drawn up to cover the price, the payment schedule, a date for completion and any penalty charges for non compliance.

TOWN PLANNING

The *Plan General de Ordenacion Urbana* is the town plan. Drawing up a plan involves both local and regional government. It involves political, social and legal change. A town plan is not a static document. It can involve the strategic planning of large developments and conversely the detailed consideration of individual planning applications.

In areas of outstanding beauty, retaining the natural charm is often a key issue with only a certain size of plot and property allowed. Asking planning authorities to change this is difficult. On the other hand planning applications are almost automatic where an area has been approved for urbanisation or general housing development.

Going to the planning department

It may be that the approval of planning applications and building permits can be influenced. A Spaniard accompanied by a local architect and builder known to the town hall planning people will gain maximum flexibility from the regulations.

Other nationalities are accustomed to obtaining planning permission for as little as a garden shed. They like to keep to the rules but find the whole planning system wearisome. Unless accompanied by a local architect or Spanish solicitor they are unlikely to be able to grapple with the complexities of the planning department.

Do you really need an architect?

The benefits of employing a good architect are in ensuring that your aspirations match your budget, sorting out any muddled thinking, designing a dream home and steering you through planning permission. The disadvantage is obviously the additional cost.

The best way to find a good architect is by personal recommendation: one who has worked on a similar project where examples of his work can be seen and references can be obtained.

The alternative is just to let the builders in. You know exactly what you want and you are confident about costs and the structural specification.

Pressures exist in Spain for the appointment of architects. It reduces the number of unscrupulous builders and unsightly designs. It removes some responsibility from the town hall to other qualified individuals.

If it goes wrong

Builders often say 'You can build anything you want here. If it goes wrong we will pay the fine.' Don't believe it. The statement may be accurate, it may be made with the best of intentions, but it is not contractually binding.

Some people build without permission. If the town hall does not object within seven years it is approved.

If permission has not been granted, or an alteration has breached the planning rules, a fine of five per cent of the alteration value is imposed, provided the alteration is satisfactory and can be legalised. Blatant breaches incur a fine of 20 per cent and the building is demolished.

RENOVATED AND RESALE – GOOD AND BAD CONTRACTS

We have said before, the contract is a linchpin of the Spanish property buying process. Further examples of contracts are highlighted in Appendices 4 and 5. The first is extremely well written by an *abogado* for an unusual property. The other, for a resale property, is designed only to benefit the agent's receipt of black money.

A good contract

The Contrato Privado de Compraventa (Full Private Contract) itself is written in a similar manner to the final *escritura*. It is clear and unambiguous. No black money is involved. Let us look at some of the interesting contents of this contract.

- Urban dwelling, in a state of ruin, situated in.....................(full address), comprising ground floor with room and corral, occupying 40 square metres.

- Mortgage in favour of.....................(bank) for twenty seven thousand Euros.

- Also to the account of the seller will be the charges derived from the cancellation of the mortgage as well as the work of amplification of the *escritura*.

In other words, this old property is situated on the edge of a Spanish town. It was a home to a family and some animals. The owner took out a mortgage to renovate the property into a modern town house with a high building specification. He then sold it. The cost of an architect to specify the new building dimensions for inclusion in the *escritura* was the responsibility of the seller.

A bad contract

The brevity of this Option Contract hides a number of important commercial points. But firstly the background. This is the resale of a relatively new holiday home by a multi-lingual Scandinavian agent, his clients being largely UK based. Let us pick out two key phrases to see what they hide.

- This property is sold to them by the agent..................with CIF number...........in representation of...............................a UK citizen, resident in this property (henceforth the seller)......... .

- The fixed agreed price is...........................Euros.

The contract states the agent acts in representation of the seller. In fact no signed document existed between the agent and seller to state this and obviously no reference is made to this in the contract. The agent could have taken the deposit and simply vanished. He did not have the right to sell the property.

The fixed agreed price of................Euros is even more misleading. It does not state what is included in the price. In fact the price did include all legal fees, taxes and the agent's commission. The net figure after these deductions is the money received by the seller. But this figure is not stated in the contract. Since the value in the *escritura* is also less than the value in the contract, the black money involved goes directly to the agent and indirectly to the *abogado* handling the deal.

The contract deviously hides all the key commercial figures. The largest and most important is the agent's commission at ten per cent of the sales price.

The buyer should always take legal advice. In this case nothing untoward occurred since both the buyer and seller were honourable people. The agent was not dishonest, but unquestionably sharp.

ONLY ONE *ABOGADO*

The conveyancing procedures in some countries have different solicitors representing the buyer and the seller. It is not necessary to have two *abogados* in Spain to complete the conveyancing. Both parties should take legal advice prior to signing the contract but where it has been drawn up by an *abogado* it can be assumed to be correct. After all, the final legal step is still to come – the notary.

SUMMARY

- Different procedures apply to the purchase of different properties.

- A fast track conveyancing procedure for new property exists in some quickly developing areas of the country.

- A resale property has a shorter procedure but checks have to be carried out before signing the contract. Does the seller have the right to sell? What are the debts or encumbrances on the property?

- Checking with the town hall for any local planning constraints is an absolute necessity before proceeding with the purchase of a property for renovation.

- Buying land, particularly rural land, can be complicated. Who owns it, where are the boundaries? Once it is purchased, what can be built on it?

- Pressures now exist for the appointment of architects for all major building projects.

- The best contract is the one drawn up by an *abogado* who is protecting the interests of his clients. Contracts drawn up by agents and builders will invariably be one sided.

11

Timeshare and Rental

TIMESHARE IS CHANGING

A classic timeshare investment is where the co-owner buys an entitlement to use a specified property for a number of weeks at a certain time of year. Additionally there is an annual fee for the management and upkeep of the property. The main principle of timeshare is that it gives quality accommodation for less than the equivalent hotel rate.

It is, however, an industry that has a bad reputation for mis-selling. This is changing. Spain introduced timeshare regulations in 1999. The highlights are:

• Restrictions on high pressure selling tactics in public places and tourist spots.

• Introducing a cooling off period of ten days during which the buyer can withdraw from the contract with no penalty.

• Written information to be supplied in the mother tongue of the buyer.

• Contract disputes are governed by Spanish law.

In the UK the product is now regulated by the Financial Services Act which means clients get protection and are able to sue the financial advisor if they believe they have been given inappropriate advice

The average timeshare buyer is a well educated home owner,

with two cars, and no children, who takes at least two holidays and two short breaks per year. The average European price for a timeshare is about 9,000 Euros for an apartment sleeping four for a purchase period of 20 to 99 years.

The timeshare market has developed a points system valuating a property according to:

- the property itself
- the number of weeks purchased
- the time of the year purchased.

Points can be used to swap the property for another owned by the same company. Timeshares are often built by large holiday companies: P&O at La Manga is a good example. Other large organisations are now entering the market, allowing the points to be spent on travel products other than accommodation.

LOOKING AT THE PROPERTY RENTAL MARKET

The rental market can be sub-divided into its segments. The first is a short term holiday rental, usually for a few weeks but lasting up to one year. The second is long term letting which in legal terms, once offered, can be for up to five years' tenancy.

Each market has different driving forces. Short term lets are driven by promotion and advertising. Long term lets, which are mainly for Spanish people, are a balance between the laws of the country giving the tenants security and landlords reward.

HOLIDAY RENTAL

There are many self catering properties for rent in Spain. Properties have been built for that purpose or are available from absentee owners. They will mainly be apartments near the sea or a golf course, or a villa in the mountains. Many detached villas with a swimming pool or rustic country houses are also available through up-market letting agents.

Although word of mouth or an advertisement in a local newspaper can often achieve the same result, the organisation of this market depends very much on a selling agent to bring the holiday tenant and landlord together. However, e-commerce and a need for the agent to offer the landlord an added value service are altering the shape of this market.

E-commerce

Short term holiday rental companies can advertise their wares more effectively through a website than by thousands of expensive brochures. Information can be assimilated very quickly making the web ideal for accessing the up-to-date availability of any holiday rental. Viewing the alternatives on a screen, checking price and availability, booking and paying by credit card take but a few clicks. E-commerce is rapidly taking over as the most effective method of booking a holiday rental.

Added value service

The landlord too is changing his requirements demanding from the letting agent a comprehensive total package to cover:

- a letting service

- emergency property maintenance and repair

- day to day management of guests' laundry, property cleaning and post collection

- personal assistance for tenants, guests and visitors to embrace collection from the airport, car hire and language translation

- arranging insurances to cover property, contents and personal health

- a legal and fiscal service to cover the payment of bills and annual tax returns.

Legal aspects

Holiday rental contracts are called *Arrienda de Temporada*. The property is furnished. The straightforward, standard contract is in Spanish or in English. With a returnable deposit required to cover any damages caused by the temporary tenant, the contract is for a specific period of time at a stated price. The renewal of the contract is at the agent's or landlord's discretion.

LONG TERM RENTAL

Properties available for long term rental are found mainly, but not exclusively, in the city. They can be furnished or unfurnished. It is an expensive method of accommodation only for those with special needs. Over a five year period it is obviously cheaper to buy and then sell than it is to rent.

Like most countries Spain has its letting law. It is called *Ley de Arrendamientos Urbanos* and commenced in 1995. The contract for a long term rental is called *Arrienda de Vivienda*. The law provides for long term rentals to be of five years' duration, thus giving the tenant a degree of security. If the landlord offers a contract of three years duration which is accepted and then the tenant wishes to stay on for another two years it is automatically renewed at the same terms. If the tenant wishes to leave after three years then the contract is terminated.

Annual rent increases in line with inflation take place during the contracted term. A new level of rent is set at the commencement of a new contract.

Which contract?

It is important to know at the outset if a short term or long term contract is being offered. Some confusion arises with contracts of one year's duration. To state the obvious: there should be a contract; it should state *temporada* or *vivienda* and the duration of the tenancy. The renewal clauses and charges should also be clearly stated.

LANDLORD'S COSTS

Irrespective of holiday or long term rental and with a similar methodology to letting a property back home, the landlord pays the community charges, the letting company's fees and chooses to declare the income for tax purposes less any property maintenance costs.

SUMMARY

- Timeshare is no longer subjected to pressure selling. The quality of accommodation offered is high.

- Short term holiday rentals are plentiful. Buying over the internet is now hugely popular.

- The landlord is obliged to offer long term rental for a period of up to five years.

- It is important to differentiate between short and long term contracts.

12

Cutting Red Tape

YOU OR THE *GESTOR*?

Spain has a reputation for red tape and bureaucracy which has its origins in duplicated decentralised government. At local level, small 'stand alone' administrative offices deal with the every day aspects of Spanish life. Little co-ordination takes place.

During your first year of life in Spain you need to undertake a number of administrative tasks. The best way to approach these tasks is to understand the principles and linkage between each government department. Then assemble all the pieces of paper and decide who is going to do it. The tasks will fall to you or the *gestor*.

DURING THE PROPERTY PURCHASE

Property administration tasks have been covered elsewhere in this book. Here is a reminder (and see Figures 14 and 15):

- Financial controls and the non-resident's certificate – see Chapter 5.

- Fiscal identification number – see Chapter 9.

- All utilities, facilities and community bills transferred into the new owner's name.

- After about six months ensure the property is registered and the *escritura* is picked up at the notary's office.

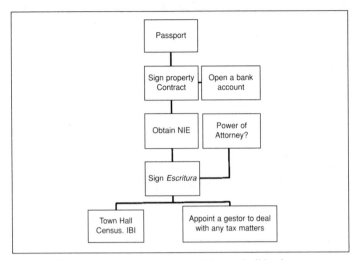

Fig. 14. Red tape decision tree – non residents – holiday home.

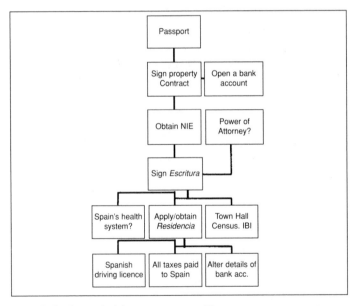

Fig. 15. Red tape decision tree – new residents.

VISITING THE TOWN HALL
Signing on the *Padron*

- Visit the town hall with your passport and the *copia simple* for the property.

- Complete some details. You are now on the census of inhabitants residing in the area administered by that particular *Ayuntamiento* (town hall).

- Persons registered will be allowed to stand and vote at elections.

- The certificado de empadronamiento (census registration certificate) is issued.

Impuesto de Bienes Inmuebles (IBI)

Popularly known as IBI this is a local tax levied on the property. It is effectively a local tax or rates payment. A receipt for the IBI payment will show the property's *catastral* reference number and the *valor catastral*, the assessed value of the property. It is necessary to visit the town hall to register the new ownership of a property and to pay the IBI, for failure to do so results in a hefty surcharge.

- Remember to look at the IBI receipts for the few years prior to purchasing a property to find out details of the charges and whether bad debts exist.

- The latest IBI receipt is given to the notary by the seller as it contains the *catastral* reference number and every sale must have it noted.

- The actual *catastral* certificate may be available from the agent or the seller.

- In addition to the property register, the *valor catastral* valuation system is effectively another system of property registration.

APPLYING FOR *RESIDENCIA*

If you intend to live permanently or to spend more than six months each year in Spain, then you are expected, the day after arriving, to begin the process of applying for *residencia*. To do this visit the Foreigners Department at the National Police Office with the following documents:

- Copy of valid passport and NIE number.

- Three passport size colour photographs.

- Evidence of belonging to a private health scheme or entitlement to enter the Spanish health system.

- A letter from the bank in Spanish, showing annual income and the current bank balance.

At the police station finger prints are taken. In about six months the new *residencia* card is issued. It is your new identity in Spain. It is renewable every five years. The passport goes into the file only to be used for international travelling. Obtaining *residencia* also necessitates a visit to the bank to change your personal details and account numbers. It means paying income tax to Spain rather than from your home country (see Chapter 13).

MEETING MOTORING REGULATIONS

The Spanish traffic department is known as *trafico*. It has a reputation for being difficult, having complex procedures and is the worst example of Spanish bureaucracy. To do this visit the appropriate *Comisaria* (Police Station) or a designated office with the following documents.

Driving licence

After obtaining your *residencia* there is a requirement to change your old licence for a new Spanish one. Recent EU regulations do not make this obligatory, and you may wish to continue to use your foreign driving licence registered and overstamped in Spain. But it has an old address and if you are a new resident of Spain it is better to have a Spanish driving licence. If anything goes wrong it makes life just that little bit easier.

- Go to the information counter at the local provincial traffic department (*Jefatura Provincial de Trafico*).

- Complete an appropriate form (*Solicitud de Carnet del Permiso de Conducir*) and present the residency card and a photocopy, the old driving licence and three passport style photographs.

- The licence is not for life. It is renewable every few years according to age. A medical examination may be necessary. It is carried out at an approved centre.

Road tax

All Spanish registered vehicles must pay road tax (*impuesto municipal sobre vehiculos de traccion mechanica*). The tax is based on the horsepower of the car. The tax levels are set by individual municipalities and can vary from town to town.

Payment is to the local town hall during a published time window (similar to IBI) after which a surcharge is applied. Unlike many other countries a tax disk is not placed inside the windscreen. Some people have avoided paying this tax for years but it catches up with them when a copy of the last receipt is required upon selling or scrapping the car.

Buying and selling

In order to buy a car in Spain it is necessary to have an NIE and a *copia simple*, or a property rental agreement, or a *residencia*. When buying a new car a registration tax of 12 per cent is levied. When buying a second-hand car a transfer tax, which reduces annually, is levied according to the age and engine size of the vehicle.

A simple agreement should be drawn up to sell a car. It should contain factual details of the buyer, the seller, details of the car, price and form of payment, the date and the appropriate signatures. It is stamped at *Trafico* to exempt the seller from future fines, accidents or taxes.

There is a two part vehicle registration, one for the details of the car and one for details of the owner. The details of the car do not alter but the part giving details of the owner alters each time there is a change. This document is called the *Permiso de Circulacion*.

It is customary when buying or selling a car to leave the administration to a garage or a *gestor*. The registration documents have to be altered, taxes paid, the town hall notified and *Trafico* informed. Quite wearisome.

ITV (technical inspection of vehicles)

After three years a bi-annual vehicle inspection, known as an ITV, is necessary. When the car is passed a sticker is placed inside the windscreen. After ten years it is an annual inspection.

Driving on foreign registered plates

A car with foreign registered plates is not permitted to stay in Spain for longer than six months. It is possible to change a car from foreign registration to Spanish registration by officially importing it. This is best done by a garage or a *gestor*.

Vehicle entrances

A garage or entrance permitting access for a vehicle to a house or building is subject to an annual tax. The entrance should display the sign *Vado Permanente*. If anyone obstructs the entrance the owners can have the vehicle legally towed away.

ENTERING THE SPANISH HEALTH SYSTEM

Temporary cover by form E111 issued by all European countries to cover illness on holiday or short visits is not an acceptable solution for Spain's new permanent residents. It is of course possible to take out medical insurance, which is the normal way of dealing with this issue. Emergencies, visits to the doctor and hospital are normally covered by the policy but medicines and dental treatment are not.

Disabled people and those over normal retiring age can gain access to the Spanish health system. They are entitled to the same medical treatment as back home.

- Obtain form E121 from the Social Security Office back home.

- Collate the *residencia* (or proof of application), the passport and a copy, and NIE.

- Go to the appropriate social security office to complete some paperwork; they will then give directions to a nominated administrative medical centre.

- The medical centre will allocate a doctor. Prescriptions and hospital care are free.

MAKING A WILL

It is not absolutely necessary, but it is advisable, to have a

Spanish will. A holiday home owner or a foreigner, resident in Spain, is permitted to dispose of his Spanish assets according to the law of his home country under a valid will. However, it would take some time to administer the Spanish estate, and it is normally recommended that a Spanish will for Spanish assets is written.

Although Spanish inheritance rules would probably differ from that of another country they are not normally applied, the national law of the deceased's home country taking precedence.
Legalising a will involves both the *abogado* and the *notary*.

Writing a will is not a problem, but advice on inheritance tax is necessary to ensure the content is correct (see Chapter 13).

SUMMARY

- Two taxes are paid at the town hall, namely rates or local tax (known as IBI) and car tax.

- It is a requirement to sign on at the town hall for the national census, the main benefit being voting rights.

- Obtaining a *residencia* is a major change for a new resident to Spain. Your old identity is partly shrugged off. It has implications for income tax payments, changes to be made at the bank and the need to have a new driving licence.

- While obtaining a Spanish driving licence is within the grasp of most people, other motoring bureaucracy is best left to the *gestor*.

- People who are disabled or over retiring age can enter the Spanish health system.

- It is recommended that a Spanish will is made out for Spanish assets.

13

Dealing with your Finances

A PERSONAL LIFE PLAN

People retiring permanently to Spain should draw up a personal
life plan statement. It can go something like this:

'While committed to a long and happy retirement in Spain, it
may be, that for whatever reason it turns out not to be a dream
and regrettably a permanent return home may be necessary. As a
consequence for the first few years at least, one foot will be kept
in Spain and one back home.' This very wise life plan has two
consequences:

- A property bolthole will be kept back home, either empty or
  rented out.

- In arranging financial plans, some of them should be based
  back home.

This 'personal life plan statement' needs to be revisited after a
year or so, with hopefully the dream realised and with both feet
now planted firmly in Spain. An adjustment to the financial mix
and the possible sale of the property back home can then take
place.

Financial advisor

It almost goes without saying that retirement planning can only
be done with a very good financial advisor, one who is strong
on pensions, investments and taxation. After 40 or so years of
working life there is only one real chance to plan a secure future

so the very best advisor is necessary.

The advisor needs to understand the taxation and investment regulations of Spain. Some financial advisors only offer advice in relation to their own country and write a disclaimer regarding the effect of their advice in Spain. This is of little help.

PLANNING YOUR PENSIONS

The principle of pensions is straightforward but constant changes in the law have allowed greater options. In an occupational pension, money has been invested by one or more parties over a number of years. The pension is paid out, usually with an inflation element, according to the rules of the scheme as set by the trustees, based on final salary and the number of years in the scheme.

Annuities, however, are a bit more complicated. An annuity is a regular income bought with a lump sum. In the last ten years annuity rates have fallen by 40 per cent. They are based on the average life expectancy and the long term yields on government bonds. Life expectancy has increased, yields have fallen – which is double bad news for annuities.

There are three types of annuity. Level annuities are paid out at the same amount for each year but the purchasing power is eroded by inflation. Escalating annuities ratchet up by a set percentage each year but the bigger the escalation the lower the income to start with. Lastly, index linked annuities can follow routes such as the Retail Price Index.

Some pensions are best left alone, some better converted to annuities. A flexible pension, taken out in the later years of life according to one's need, is excellent. A choice of pension is a major decision. Once done, that is it, for the rest of your life.

PLANNING YOUR INVESTMENTS

Investments are more flexible although each one should be entered into with a long-term strategy. Investments are about risk, with risk being relative to each person. Reward follows risk, it is the law of economics.

Risk can be categorised, ranging from inflation risk to gambling risk, but most investments focus on geographical, sectional and equity risk. Geographical risk involves a part of the world such as the UK, Europe or the USA. Sectional risk involves investing in a sector such as technology, retail or food. Equity risk relates to the investment type such as bonds, shares or unit trusts.

At the bottom of the risk ladder are building societies, corporate bonds and government stocks. Going up the risk ladder are tracker funds that mirror the FTSE 100, and shares in companies. Near the top are overseas investments, or themed investments such as technology stocks. At the top are volatile futures dealings.

INVESTING IN SPAIN

A variety of investments are available for the ex-pat in Spain. They are advertised in the weekly newspapers. In addition to conventional investments they range from dabbling in the futures market, buying up endowment policies and purchasing offshore unit trusts or bonds.

With-profits bonds

One of the more sound investments is an offshore with-profits investment bond being a tax efficient single life insurance policy, offered by a number of reputable investment companies with offices in Luxembourg, the Isle of Man or Guernsey. There is a choice of investment and the opportunity of regular withdrawals. The key is the investment stays in the offshore geographical location, the gains not being affected by the place of residence. Responsibility for the declaration of withdrawals rests with the investor.

Financial legalisation

A word of warning. The law of Europe is changing. Offshore banks are now obliged to disclose the interest gained in accounts to the tax authorities in the country where the account holder resides. A few European countries have opted to levy a witholding tax. Some people speculate that further legislation may occur, limiting the benefits of offshore investments.

Inheritance trusts

Protection from taxation and inheritance legalisation can be achieved by setting up an offshore trust fund, which initially sounds expensive and complex, but in practice can be achieved simply by organisations specialising in this type of work. Protection of a property from inheritance tax is not possible under a trust.

DEALING WITH PERSONAL TAXATION

Personal taxation is at the best of times complicated. In that context the Spanish taxman does not disappoint. As you would expect the tax system is also ever changing. Most taxes in Spain are based on self assessment where the individual is liable to report and calculate any tax due. Since we have difficulties doing this at the best of times the average new resident or non resident in Spain has little chance of getting this correct. Enter the *gestor*, who will not only perform these administrative tasks but may even suggest legitimate methods of tax avoidance. See Figure 16 for comparisons with other European countries.

Spain is not a tax haven. Its level of taxation is, however, generally low. Government taxes are collected by the *Agencia Estatal de Administracion Tributaria* but it is commonly called the *Hacienda*. The Spanish tax year is 1 January to 31 December. Tax returns must be presented between 1 May and 20 June.

There are four main taxes administered by the *Haciendia*

COUNTRY	Gross earnings Euros per annum	% tax deduction	Net deduction Euros per annum
Belgium	44,300	42	18,600
Denmark	42,100	38	16,000
Germany	48,300	38	18,350
Finland	30,400	37	11,250
Sweden	31,100	37	11,470
Austria	41,200	36	14,830
Italy	38,000	35	13,300
Holland	39,200	31	12,150
France	38,200	29	11,100
Portugal	25,500	28	7,150
Greece	19,700	25	4,925
UK	34,100	25	8,525
Luxembourg	46,500	23	11,650
Spain	30,400	22	6,690
Ireland	25,600	18	4,600

Fig. 16. European taxation levels.
Tax and Social Security Contributions expressed as a percentage of gross earnings demonstrating Spain's low earning and taxation level.
Source: William Mercer

which the resident and non resident will have to deal with. The rules differ from resident to non resident.

- Income tax (*impuesto sobre la renta de las personas físicas*)
- Capital gains which is calculated under income tax
- Wealth tax (*impuesto sobre el patrimonio*)
- Inheritance tax (*impuesto sobre sucesiones y donaciones*).

Government business taxes, employment taxes and value added tax (IVA) are not considered here. Local taxes such as IBI, plus valia and car tax have been covered earlier.

To complete tax returns, some documentation is necessary:

- Details of an NIE number, address, age and marital status.

- Proof of income plus a year end bank statement to show any interest paid and average balance. The interest is added to income and the average balance is part of the world wide assets for wealth tax.

- A recent IBI receipt (see page 146) which will contain the property value (valor catastral) which is used to calculate additional property taxes known as *Patrimonio and Renta Tax* (Wealth Tax and Unearned income Tax). *Renta* is nothing to do with renting out the property. It is a separate tax that is paid with the Patrimonio.

- Receipts for any tax paid in another country.

- Details of any changes in stocks, shares, investments or insurance policies.

- Details of any changes in major assets such as property (such as mortgages and extensions), boats and artefacts.

INCOME TAX

Resident

A Spanish resident is one who spends more than six months per year in the country, who has a *residencia* and has notified the tax authorities back home of their departure on form P85. This triggers entry into the Spanish tax system who have a treaty with other European countries designed to ensure that income that has already been taxed in one country is not taxed again in another country. One exception – a UK government pension is taxed in the UK but not in Spain.

Income tax is payable on both earned and unearned worldwide income such as wages, pensions, property and investment income.

A number of allowances can be deducted from gross income. These are mainly related to personal and family allowances, social security payments and relief for the wage earner.

Residents are taxed on a sliding scale from 15 to 40 per cent. A tax rate of 15 per cent for example is applied to a net taxable income of 3,600 Euros and 38 per cent for example is applied to a net taxable income of 40,000 Euros.

Non resident

Income tax for non residents is simpler and more brutal. Income is taxed at a flat rate 25 per cent with no allowances. A non-resident is liable for Patrimonio and Renta Tax. Patrimonio is calculated at 0.2% of the valor castral. *Renta* is calculated as 25% of 1.1% of the rateable value of a property. Together these taxes work out at half a percent of the property value. A resident does not pay *Patrimonio and Renta Tax* except on second and subsequent properties.

.

CAPITAL GAINS

Liability to capital gains applies to residents and non residents. Capital gains are payable on the profit from the sale of assets in Spain such as property, stocks and shares, antiques, art and jewellery. Since most ex-pats will have arranged their investments free of tax, capital gains in practice should only apply to property. A capital gain is based on the difference between the purchase price and the selling price of the property, less the costs of buying and selling, and costs of improvement.

Residents

If the property has been owned for less than two years the gain is added to income and taxed accordingly. If the property has been owned for more than two years the gain is reduced by an inflation factor and roll over relief allowed on the purchase of another property. Tax is payable at the individual's income tax rate with an fixed deduction before payment. For those over 65 years of age the gain is tax free.

Non residents

For the non resident the gain is taxed at a flat 35 per cent. The two year ownership rule and inflation factor allowance still apply. Roll over relief for the purchase of another property and age exemption do not.

WEALTH TAX

Residents

Spanish residents are required to pay wealth tax on their worldwide assets less any liabilities. The assets are defined as property, vehicles, jewellery, investments and cash in hand at the bank. Liabilities include mortgages and other debts. The first 110,000 Euros are free of tax (double that for a couple) and thereafter taxed on a sliding scale commencing at 0.2 per cent.

Non residents

Non residents again incur harsher penalties. They pay wealth tax at the same rate as residents on their Spanish assets but have no tax free allowance.

INHERITANCE TAX

Inheritance tax is certainly the most complicated of the taxes and needs specialised advice to legitimately reduce any liability upon death.

- Inheritance tax is payable if the recipient is a resident of Spain or the assets being passed on death are a property in Spain.

- Inheritance tax is paid by the beneficiaries and not by the deceased's estate.

- Inheritance tax starts on a sliding scale after a fixed allowance of 16,000 Euros per recipient.

- There is no exemption between husband and wife for the joint ownership of property. In many countries a property can be held in joint names. If one person dies the property passes automatically to the other person. This is not the case in Spain where each person holds an equal share which upon the death of one person is subject to inheritance tax and succession law.

- The cornerstone of avoiding inheritance tax is to have a Spanish will for Spanish assets, good financial advice and the possibly use of an inheritance trust.

Exempting property

The value of a property can be reduced by 95 per cent for the purposes of inheritance tax when the principal residence is bequeathed to a spouse, parent or child who have been living with the deceased two years prior to death and the inheritors own the property ten years from the date of death.

Yet another method of reducing inheritance tax is the peculiarly Spanish method of setting up an *usufructo* (a life interest). In this situation the ownership of the house can pass to the children leaving the life interest holders free to live in the property for the rest of their lifetime. Legitimate this may be, easy to set up, but perhaps more suited to passing down the family home from generation to generation.

SUMMARY

- Drawing up a personal life plan statement and obtaining financial advice from someone with knowledge of Spanish taxation is a useful precursor for the life of a new resident.

- Investing in Spain gives an opportunity to consider the advantages of offshore funds.

- Everyone pays tax. It is complex. Compared with other countries, personal taxation levels are low.

- Income tax which incorporates capital gains, wealth tax and inheritance tax all have to be dealt with.

- One significant difference lies with the joint ownership of property. On the death of one person the share does not automatically pass tax free to the other person.

14

Learning about Culture

WHAT IS CULTURE?

Why do we say the Germans are boring, the Italians hot headed, the Swiss secretive, the French awkward and the Dutch rather nice? This is a description of people but not the culture of a nation, which can be defined as 'civilisation, customs, life style and society'.

A Spanish guide taking a coach tour of Germans, Scandinavians, Swiss and some British to Gibraltar described it as 'typically English'. When pressed he said the pubs, the fish and chips shops were a way of life in England. That's how others see the Brits! It may not be liked, but that's how it is. Incidentally Gibraltar, in addition to pubs and fish and chip shops, is full of tax free electrical and liquor outlets. The tourist attractions play patriotic songs such as ' Land of Hope and Glory'.

What we are after is a flavour of Spain. Not the artificial tourist Spain of sun, sea, sand and sangria, but the real Spain, of the urban and rural dweller, of Andulucia, Aragon and Asturias.

ES BUENO DESCANSAR Y NO HACER NADA DESPUES!

Spaniards have a zest for living and commonly put as much energy into enjoying their lives as they do into their work. Time is flexible, many people organise their work to fit the demands of their social life, rather than let themselves be ruled by work or the clock. All big cities have a buzz and all rural areas have their tractors and carts, but two undisputed facts support the view that a slower pace of life prevails in Spain. One is the intense midday summer heat which makes even small movement impossible. The other is *mañana*, a deeply rooted Spanish attitude which frustrates the British and does permanent damage to German relationships. *Mañana* means tomorrow or perhaps the day or week after, but certainly not today. Spaniards know they do it. They also know it causes difficulties but in truth it is a way of life that says 'time is not important, tomorrow will do'.

There is an old Spanish proverb which goes along the lines 'It is good to do nothing and rest afterwards' (*es bueno descansar y no hacer nada despues*). While this cannot be applied in all situations, and indeed many may take offence, there are times where the words are wholly appropriate.

RELIGION

Catholicism is still an influence over Spanish society. Although church attendance is falling, on a Sunday around midday, families can be seen dressed in their best attire strolling home from their place of worship. The images of saints watch over shops, bars and drivers' cabs. Traditional fiestas mark church feasts.

THE FAMILY GROUP

The family group is strong with sometimes two or three generations living within one house. The Spanish love of children is well known. Children will be beautifully dressed with a confidence that befits offspring in the new millennium. Mother and father will be proud parents with a deep sense of honour. Grandparents will be friendly, courteous, generous, not fully comprehending the staggering changes which have taken place since their childhood.

The young macho male will study in the evening for personal

advancement, will watch football and own a fast scooter. The beautiful dark haired *senorita* will be slim, wear flared trousers, and somehow be one foot taller and one foot narrower than her mother. Traditionally the man expects his wife to be the provider of love and affection and to keep a clean home worthy of her husband. But this is changing fast, with Spanish women seeking more freedom and equality alongside their more worldly sisters.

At the weekend the family group will come together along with an assortment of aunts and uncles. With military precision, in a long line, they will make their way to the edge of the sea, each carrying an essential item for the day's outing. Parents will be first, loaded down with food, grandparents next with deck chairs, uncles with umbrellas, aunts and children with buckets, spades and balls. They will have a great time with a babble of excited conversation, interspersed with a shout, a wave of the hand, a shake of the shoulder, or a kiss in greeting or farewell.

HOW THE SPANISH PARTY

Fiestas

Fiestas celebrate a national religious occasion or a local thanksgiving where towns and cities come to a stop as men, women and children dress up to enjoy themselves aided by a plentiful supply of food, wine and laughter. Processions with music start the evening, dancing and singing follow. Fireworks close the evening with a loud colourful bang. Each fiesta has its own distinctive character – sounds, colours, flavours, smells, costumes, rituals and a typical dish. There are celebrations for the dead and the living. Some fiestas appease the forces of nature. Others drive out evil spirits. Often they are based on historical events or include medieval or ancient customs. There is always a fiesta somewhere. They can last for a day, a week or a fortnight.

Perhaps the best known fiesta is the one celebrating the re-conquest of the Moors by the Christians, held at Alcoy near

Alicante but also replicated in many other Spanish towns in that region. Throughout the world there are many colourful processions but few can compare with the medieval pageantry which is accompanied by the music of brass instruments and loud kettle drums, as the marchers slowly sway rhythmically in the early darkness of a summer's evening.

Flamenco

Flamenco has its home in Andalucia, being traditionally performed by gypsies. It is more than just a dance, being an expression of life, improvising to the rhythm of the guitar. Just as important, however, is the beat created by hand clapping and by the dancers feet in high-heeled shoes. Castanets, solo singing and graceful hand movements are used to express feelings of pain, sorrow or happiness. Flamenco is best seen in Sevilla, modified for mass audiences and tourists, but still a fiery individualistic performance.

Bullfighting

In the southern cities of Cordoba, Granada and Sevilla a bullfighting poster is a common sight. Indeed, in some shops it is possible to have your own name printed on one. This is where the glamour ends. Hemingway understood bullfighting but modern Europeans do not, seeing it as a cruel bloody sport, shocking and not for the faint-hearted. The Spanish see it as an art, a colourful spectacle where the skill of the bullfighter is pitched against the raw aggression of the bull. 'Six brave bulls' the poster reads, but the bull does not win, sometimes dying, at teatime, on live national television.

Bull running

Bull running, made famous in Pamplona but also practised in many Spanish towns, offers the bull better odds. In this case the young macho male is the one in danger. The bulls are let loose in the streets of the town. Aspiring men run to avoid their horns. A few are injured and some die.

EATING OUT

Food is important. Spaniards enjoy café life. Like the French they live to eat, not eat to live.

Breakfast is a coffee with bread or a croissant. There are three popular types of coffee. *Café solo* is a small cup of strong coffee, not for the thirsty. *Café con leche* is coffee with milk. *Café americano* is a large cup without milk. *Churos* – a doughnut type fried pastry with hot chocolate – forms a traditional breakfast of mega calories.

Lunch takes place between 2.00 pm and 4.00 pm and outside the home will consist of *tapas* or alternatively a light three course meal with wine and bread. The choices for *menu del dia* are chalked up on a blackboard outside the restaurant (see Figure 17). The starter (*primero*) is soup, salad or pasta, the main course (*segundo*) is meat or fish and the sweet (*postre*) is fruit, ice cream or flan.

Dinner is late – 8.00 pm to 10.00 pm. It is usually a repeat of lunch, but with a bit more wine and a bit less food. No one wants to go to bed on a full stomach.

Tapas

The *tapas* bar is unique to Spain. Rows of dishes are arranged in a chilled cabinet in front of the customer. A choice is made, with bread and coffee or wine, to be eaten at the bar, at an adjacent table or at a table on the pavement or street. The offerings are made by the proprietor or by a local food preparation unit. They comprise tortilla, spicy meat balls, big plump olives, sausages, fried aubergines, egg salad, courgettes, spicy potatoes, liver, cheese, serrano ham, sardines, prawns in garlic, anchovies, mussels, fried squid, calamares, sepia, and small fish in olive oil.

Fig. 17. A typical menu.

A good example of simple food, at a fixed price, to be enjoyed with some wine. This meal would be served at a café, bar or restaurant. It would be eaten by workmen, office staff, tourists and residents alike.

Eight Euros for a *menu del día*, or for three *tapas* and some wine, is excellent value for money. Glass in hand, soaking up the warmth of the sun and the people, watching the world go by, puts one very close to the seven heavens of the cosmos depicted at the Alhambra in Granada.

CUSTOMS, THE ARTS AND OPERA

Outside the restaurant, in the main square or along the promenade the evening *paseo* commences with young girls and boys, parents and grandparents strolling in a leisurely manner.

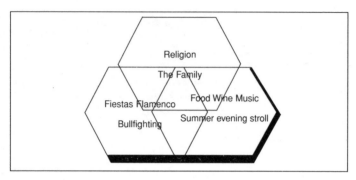

Fig. 18. Traditional Spanish culture.

For some it is gentle exercise in the cool of the evening, for others a prelude to a good night out, for the spectators it is an entertainment.

In villages chairs are placed in the narrow streets, oblivious to passing traffic, as occupants emerge from their houses, to talk and gossip about the day's events.

Spain has many buildings of great architectural interest. Each town has its main square with a town hall. The country is famous for its ornate furniture, metalwork, sculpture and ceramics. Culture and the arts are linked. Famous artists include Dali, Goya and Velazquez. Placido Domingo and Jose Carreras represent opera.

THE SHOPPING EXPERIENCE

Spain does not have the equivalent of a Boots, Marks & Spencer, Dixons, WH Smith or a JJD Sports. With the exception of grocery groups, few shopping chains exist. The Spanish shopping experience is absolutely different with specialist small family run outlets forming the bulk of sales activity.

Why is there a difference between Spain and the multiple retail outlets of northern Europe? Well, remember it is a large country with a low population density, which in turn gives rise to high distribution costs. The nature of retailing has as a consequence many outlets, with high price points and little discounting.

But in the cool of the evening, with a stop for a *café con leche* or a *tapas*, indulging in a multilingual conversation with the occupants at the next table, shopping can still be a pleasurable activity.

Tiendas

The smaller *tiendas* (shops) are cheerful, friendly, helpful places where the owners and assistants are anxious to please. This is also where the annoying Spanish characteristic of 'not forming queues' is seen at its worst. People push and shove to the front to be served. This is best dealt with patience as the perpetrators of this behaviour are often elderly who seem to think that their advanced years entitle them to non-queuing privileges. Alternatively say *'perdone'* and address the sales assistant, who usually knows what is happening.

Opening hours for *tiendas* vary between summer and winter, but normally are 9.30 am to 1.30 pm and 4.30 pm to 7.30 pm Monday to Friday, plus a Saturday morning. The afternoon siesta seems inappropriate in winter but essential in summer, when the shops open later, as no one wishes to go shopping during the intense heat. There is, however, pressure to change this custom from businesses and other Europeans. Banks and some organisations open at 8.00 am and close at 2.30 pm. Holiday resorts, restaurants and hypermarkets, open 7 days a week, 12 hours a day, have already squeezed the siesta out of existence.

The *tienda* retailing backbone is highly specialised.

Bread shop	– *La panaderia*
Butcher	– *La carniceria*
Cake shop	– *La pasteleria*
Chemist	– *La farmacia*

Clothes shop	– *La tienda de ropa*
Delicatessen	– *La charcuteria*
Fruit shop	– *La fruteria*
Fishmonger	– *La pescaderia*
Grocer	– *La tienda de comestibles*
Hairdresser	– *La peluqueria*
Ironmonger	– *La ferreteria*
Laundrette	– *Lavanderia*
Newspaper stand	– *El quiosco*
Shoe shop	– *La zapateria*
Travel agent	– *Agency de viajes*
Tobacconist	– *El tabac*

Hypermarkets

French owned hypermarkets such as Carrefour and Intermarche, dominate food retailing. Smaller German supermarkets such as Lidl and Aldi compete on price but not on product range. Spanish companies such as Mercadona are now gaining a firm foothold. Hypermarket shopping is an experience not to be missed, with everything possible being sold under one roof: clothes, footwear, garden plants and equipment, sports goods, bicycles, electrical goods, hi-fi, furniture, DIY, motoring accessories, kitchenware, toys and books. The food hall has a massive product range. The fruit and vegetables are highly colourful. The delicatessen counter is staggering in its variety of sausage and cheese. The fish counter is laden down with salmon, trout, mussels, skate, mackerel and a whole range of unrecognisable species. The wine, spirits, soft drinks and bottled water section stretches for miles. These hypermarkets have 40 to 60 checkouts. Key staff are equipped with roller skates to get from point to point. Franchised within the same building are restaurants, banks, jewellers, newsagents and the National Lottery.

Clothing

Regrettably there is only one major, but famous, clothing chain store in Spain – El Corte Ingles. It has a similar marketing style to other European retailers, selling mainly male and female clothing together with books, CDs, electrical goods, computers, kitchen ware and sports equipment. Price points are similar to or higher than the rest of Europe with only occasional sales (*rebajas*). With the exception of a large number of international sports brands, clothing is not fashionable. It is conservative in taste, for Spain is not yet a fashion centre; its citizens stick to fairly traditional styles.

European chain stores, like European banks, have only a few outlets in major cities. The marketplace may be penetrated by individual foreign brands but not by foreign retailers. Where they do exist they tend to be a poor relation of their national parents.

Open air markets

There are a profusion of mobile open-air markets, often stopping normal activity in a town for one day of each week. People flock from kilometres around to buy hams, fish, fresh fruit and vegetables. Clothing too is sold together with some ceramics and leather goods. Beware of purchasing designer items, watches and jewellery as they may be branded fakes.

Bargaining takes place, but it is an unnatural custom for northern Europeans. Want to bargain? Express an interest in an item. Haggle on price. Say 'no' and walk away. The stall owner comes after you. That's when you get the low price, not before.

The hustle and bustle can be of some interest, but be cautious. Pickpockets, operating in gangs of two or three, are often present at open-air markets.

Mercado central

The central market is run by the local council. Most towns have one. They are efficient, clean, hygienic purveyors of fish, meat, pastries, fruit and vegetables, a traditional alternative to supermarket shopping. Little English is spoken but a smile accompanies each purchase.

'Algo mas?'   (Anything else)
'Eso es todo.'   (That's all)
'Gracias.'   (Thank you)

Strangely, Spanish fresh fruit and vegetables have to be purchased with care. Locally grown produce in season is cheap and available all year long, but of course like all European countries Spain exports most of its Class I produce. Quality produce is better purchased from the *fruteria* at the *mercado central* than from the supermarket.

Tabac

One other national institution has to be mentioned – The *tabac*, the state owned tobacco shop selling all brands of cigarettes, cigars and tobacco at very low prices: 20 Euros for 200 cigarettes is quite normal. It is fairly obvious from these prices many people still smoke. In bars and restaurants, shops and public places, the cigarette is still part of the Spanish way of life. The *tabac* has other functions. It also provides government forms for taxation and sells postage stamps. Never stand in a long queue at the main post office for stamps when a *tabac* is nearby.

BUYING WINE AND OLIVE OIL

Wine

The best buys in Spain, apart from tobacco, colourful ceramics and leather products, are undoubtedly wine and olive oil, both agricultural products from tightly regulated industries.

The Mediterranean countries of Italy, France and Spain all produce good quality wine under various climatic conditions. Spain produces excellent wines but their product marketing has been poor, leaving France holding the premium market and Spain operating at the bottom end. Tighter government regulations have seen a continuous rise in wine quality but not in their marketing strategy.

There are about 55 officially designated wine-producing areas, all individually indicated by a small map on the label on the back of each bottle. Each area has a number of measurable standards specified for the product.

There are broadly three main wine-producing areas: the north, of which Rioja is by far the best known; the central area best known for La Mancha wines, and the southern area, which produces aperitif wines and sherry.

Rioja is a strong red wine comparable to any French product but considerably cheaper. In the best tradition of wine regions its annual vintage is classified as poor, normal, good, very good or excellent.

No one makes a fuss about drinking wine. At an equivalent cost to a soft drink or a bottle of water, it is the natural accompaniment to a meal. Branded wine, with an individual number on the back of the bottle, blended house wines, *vino de mesa* (table wines), young wines or supermarket brands at two to three Euros per bottle are all exceptional value for money.

Olive oil

There are 400 million olive trees in Spain with 80 per cent grown in Andalucia. Driving around Cordoba and Granada you can see fields and fields, acres and acres of olive trees. The experts in Brussels say there are too many; olive oil production is too high. *Aceite de Oliva* (olive oil) is used in cooking, in a salad dressing and as a substitute for butter and margarine.

Some people say it is olive oil, together with fresh fruit, vegetables, and fish which makes the Spanish diet so healthy.

SUMMARY

- The culture of a country is not just its people, but also its attitudes, life style and customs.

- So what is Spanish culture? It is a romantic mix of fiesta, flamenco and music, flavoured with good food and wine, coloured with friendly people. And of course . . . where time is not important.

- The pace of life is generally slower in Spain.

- The family is a very strong group. They love to party. Fiestas and eating out are top of the list. Socialising and just talking come next.

- Small family shops form the backbone of retailing. Massive French hypermarkets sell just about everything.

- Open-air markets are big and noisy but have little to commend them. The *mercado central* offers good quality produce. The *tabac* is an unusual feature of life in Spain.

- Wine and olive oil offer good quality at a low price.

15

Living Life to the Full

MOTORING

Roads

Motoring in Spain is easy. It is a big country. Driving in the country is still a pleasure.

Spain's motorways are known as *autopistas* or *autovias*, both characterised by blue signposting and built to a high standard. *Autopistas* are toll roads. The other roads in Spain are identified by the sign '*Red de Carreteras del Estado*' (the red roads of the country), the *Carreteras Nacionales* (letter N on maps), and the narrower *Carreteras Comarcales* (letter C). They all tend to be busy, single lane roads, often taking traffic more suited to the expensive toll roads.

On major roads each kilometre is marked with a number being the distance radiating from Madrid. In the provinces it is the distance from the provincial capital. These kilometer markers are often used as convenient meeting points or used to establish the location of a building.

On the spot fines are handed out for breaking speed limits, which are:

autopistas	120 km/h
autovias	120 km/h
Carreteras Nacionale	90 km/h
Carreteras Comarcales	60 km/h

Gasolina (petrol), *gasoleo* (diesel), and *Gasolina sin Plomo* (unleaded petrol) are available everywhere at prices well below the European average. Indeed diesel is only about 60 per cent of the most expensive European price.

The number of filling stations are increasing rapidly. They also sell newspapers, food and snacks. Motorway services are poor and infrequent, generally recognised as the worst in Europe.

Driving on the right side of the road

The most obvious motoring difference is of course left hand drive cars and driving on the right hand side of the road. There are other differences:

- Going around roundabouts in an anti clockwise direction – be careful, in some situations the car already on the roundabout does not have the right of way.

- If going in the wrong direction on a major road, it is possible to change direction when the sign *Cambio de Sentido* appears.

- When turning left at a busy junction, it may be necessary to turn right first and then cross the carriageway.

- Two flashing amber lights means 'slow down, danger ahead'.

- Respect the narrow inside lane, it is for scooters.

- Seat belts are of course compulsory.

- All vehicle documents such as insurance details, car registration and technical ITV sheets should be kept in the car for inspection by the police if necessary.

Accidents

Unfortunately Spain has one of the highest accident rates in

Europe. A high incidence of foreign drivers is one significant reason. Poor roads and alcohol are other major reasons. One further characteristic stands out – speed. Spanish drivers are similar to the Italians and drivers on the Paris ring road – they all drive in a fast, aggressive manner. At slip roads, where they join major roads, no quarter is given or asked by the incoming drivers. Judging speed, slipping into a small gap between moving traffic, can be quite frightening.

Driving a foreign registered car temporarily in Spain requires a green card, a bail bond, a national identity sticker on the back of the car, two red triangles, spare bulbs and a first aid kit. The headlights may need to be adjusted. In the case of an accident, the insurance certificate, driving licence and passport need to be kept handy. Permanently driving a right hand drive car in Spain is not a good idea.

Purchasing a car (*el coche*)

The market for the purchase of new cars is similar across Europe. Large dealers sell new and some second hand cars at very competitive list prices with a good after-sales service. Since dealerships are monitored by the car manufacturers the service is efficient, well organised and, above all, reputable.

Although things are changing, product pricing in Spain is not affected by discounting or special offers except where the offer is directly from the manufacturer. The sales price is mainly from a published list price. Cars in Spain are slightly cheaper than some of their European counterparts due to lower purchase taxes.

Given Spain's geographical location and the ownership of car manufacturing plants in Valencia, the popular brands are Seat and Ford. French products come next. Quality German cars are popular. The market penetration of small Far Eastern cars is high.

Regrettably the second hand car market does not enjoy a good reputation with the usual unsavoury dealers in evidence, some of whom are British. Fortunately the quality of a modern second hand car is high. It is price, poor administration, a lack of customer service and dishonesty which gives this market its poor reputation.

The market for second hand cars is unusual. A large number of year old rental cars, with relatively low mileages, are sold through the second hand market each year. Trade-ins for new dealership purchases are also sold through second hand outlets.

There is a third market for cars through the small ads in weekly newspapers. For a first time buyer in Spain the advice is to tread carefully. The risk of a poor product or incorrect paperwork is too high.

Insurance

Insurance companies offer the usual cover with options such as voluntary excess, no claims bonus and passenger insurance. One good additional extra is breakdown insurance which provides for transportation of the car and occupants in the event of breakdown or illness.

Linea Directa (Direct Line), a leading UK insurance provider, in a joint venture with a Spanish bank, is the fastest growing car insurance group in Spain.

DEALING WITH THE POST

Correos, the national postal service of Spain, is easily identified by the yellow signs outside each post office. Yellow is also the colour of mail vans, delivery scooters and mail boxes. Mail to and from Europe is automatically sent air mail. Delivery of mail in Spain can be slow.

Try to avoid going into some Spanish post offices. They can be small and dark with long, slow moving queues. Go to the *tabac* for stamps. One price covers all EU countries:

'*Diez sellos para Europa, por favor*' (ten stamps for Europe, please).

Letters are delivered to a household door or American style to a driveway gate. On urbanisations all the post boxes are grouped together beside a focal point such as the swimming pool. It is necessary to go to the post office to collect parcels or registered mail when identification may be required.

The post office offers a range of services. Registered or express mail, parcel post, redirection, private boxes and banking are all available.

All is not well with the Spanish postal system. Delays and strikes are common. Mail Boxes Etc, a USA company, has a number of offices in Spain. Although still dependent on the services of Correos it operates independently for overnight international parcel delivery through companies such as UPS and FedEx. It also offers a mail box service, shipping and packing, fax printing and photocopying. It sells office supplies and stamps. This enlightened company is refreshing to deal with but its activities are restricted by protectionism offered to the state postal system.

GETTING THE NAME AND ADDRESS CORRECT

Spanish names are important. A mother's maiden name is added to the end of a full name; women do not change their name when they marry; the formal prefix of *Don* or *Dona* is introduced at the start of a name.

Senor Don John Frederick Smith King is simply Mr John Smith with a middle name Frederick and a mother's maiden name King. He is married to Senora Dona Maria Dolores Sanchez Vicario. Got it? Who is Conchita Smith Sanchez? Yes, correct, their daughter Conchita. Telephone books can be fun!

An accurate address is also important:

Sr Smith
Calle Madrid 27, 2
03189 Orihuela Costa
Alicante

Translated this means:

Name			Mr Smith	
Number	street	floor	27 Madrid St,	2nd Floor
Post code	town		03189	Orihuela Costa
Province			Alicante	

The zip code 03189 is made up of 03 as the province number and 189 the post office number.

COMING TO TERMS WITH COMMUNICATIONS

Television

This medium is now dominated by digital TV. Most ex-pats want to tune into English language programmes. These can be found on Spanish, BBC and Sky digital systems via a satellite dish. Urbanisations may offer a better selection of English, French, German, Scandinavian and Spanish channels through an underground cable system.

There are a number of Spanish television stations but Spanish television is dominated by pay-as-you-view programming of films and football, together with the standard news, documentaries, music, soaps and old films.

Radio

A mention should be made of radio. Spanish FM stàtions are available by the dozen, all featuring some music and endless chatter. More interesting, however, are the popular UK based FM stations available by satellite. These stations are received by digital receiver or by a separate FM cable. It is not possible to forget Mr Wogan; after all who wants to escape that friendly voice.

Telephoning

Telefonica (the Spanish telephone company) charges for calls, line rental and telephone rental. The tariffs are for local, national and international calls. Time tariffs exist for peak, normal and night time. Peak times are 8.00 am to 8.00 pm Monday to Friday, and 8.00 am to 2.00 pm on Saturday. Emergency telephone numbers are published in the white pages of the telephone directory and also in English language weekly newspapers. Telephone number 1092 gets the local police, 1004 the operator.

Telefonica has limited competition for its landline service but like most major companies meets this competition head on with price reductions and special offers. MoviStar is the mobile phone company of Telefonica which has far greater competition from Vodaphone and other companies.

Newspapers

These are of great interest. Local, national and international; daily, weekly and monthly; Spanish and English; expensive, cheap and free publications, all clog the news-stands. Spanish daily newspapers are mainly middle class. *El Pais* (The Country) and *El Mundo* (The World) have lots of pages aimed at the serious reader and are cracking good value for money. At the bottom end of the Spanish daily press the content is devoted solely to football.

All the European daily newspapers are available. They are printed in Spain but cost three times more than the national edition. Weekend newspapers also have some sections missing. The best reads for the ex-pat are the locally printed English language weekly newspapers. They are a good blend of national and local news, lots of gossip, information and adverts. Indeed some of the small ads are reminiscent of standing inside a central London telephone box.

Popular English language books are more difficult to find but large and small English bookshops do exist. Specialist titles are best purchased through e-commerce.

THREE POLICE FORCES

The *Guardia Civil* (National Guard) mainly police rural areas. Their uniform is olive green. They deal with traffic and traffic offences.

The *Policia Nacional* (National Police), who wear a blue uniform, operate in towns with a population greater than 30,000. They are concerned with crime.

Policia Municipal are local police. They also dress in blue. They operate independently in a town and also have a separate section for traffic control.

All three police forces carry truncheons. The *Guardia Civil* and *Policia Nacional* carry guns. They are tolerant and polite except when dealing with major crime.

HOW FOREIGNERS PARTY

We already know how the Spanish party. Fiestas and bullfighting. Eating at the *tapas* bar. Watching the evening *paseo* or just talking. Do resident or non-resident foreigners party the same way? Do they shrug off their old habits and party as Spaniards? No, not really.

About 12 million people whose native tongue is English will visit or reside in Spain in any year. The European Commission, in a survey, found that only three per cent speak Spanish. A lack of command of a second language puts them at a severe disadvantage when communicating and integrating into the Spanish way of life (see Figure 20).

The influx of foreign residents is not evenly spread throughout Spain. Some towns have developed as foreign enclaves. Denia, for example, has a high proportion of German residents. New urbanisations, when built, are marketed heavily in one country or another but not evenly across all countries.

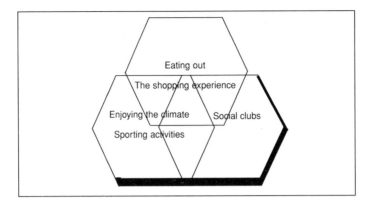

Fig. 19. Culture of the new residents.

Retired foreign residents have lots of free time, more than the average Spaniard. This time is filled according to customs acquired back home and not to the cultural activities existing in Spain. All this leads to two facts:

- Foreigners do not generally integrate into the Spanish way of life.

- Each nationality tend to stick together, developing sporting activities and social habits based on a former life back home.

EL TIEMPO LIBRE

Let us go out. Let us develop some leisure activities and meet some new friends. The Spanish call it *el tiempo libre* (free time).

The diverse geographical nature of Spain, with its mountains, woodlands, beaches and sea, gives a wonderful backdrop for spare time activities. Golf clubs, sports centres, bowling greens, gymnasiums, swimming pools and tennis clubs are all striving to make better use of our leisure time. The newcomer faces a bewildering choice of activities only handicapped by the ageing process, which probably rules out bull fighting, bungee jumping

183

Food	Leisure	Entertainment	Shops
1. Tea bags	1. Pubs	1. Cinema	1. M & S
2. Chocolate	2. Countryside	2. British news	2. Boots
3. Fresh milk	3. British culture	3. EastEnders	3. Corner shop
4. Marmite	4. Football	4. Theatre	4. Newsagent
5. Baked beans	5. Cricket	5. Friends	5. Selfridges
6. Bacon	6. Wimbledon	6. Magazines	6. HMV
7. Crisps	7. Cycling	7. British radio	7. Oasis
8. Fish & chips	8. Evening classes	8. Family	8. Next
9. Cheddar cheese	9. Quiz nights	9. Street markets	9. Oddbins

Fig. 20. What expatriate Brits miss the most.

The most recent figures from the Office of National Statistics (NOS) show 268,000 people left the UK in the past ten years to live or work abroad. Fifty-six per cent leave for work related reasons. This survey analysed what British people missed most when living abroad. The survey embraced Abbey National customers conducting business from their Jersey, Isle of Man, Spanish, Dubai and Hong Kong offices. While there is no doubt about the accuracy of the survey, all the food items can be bought in the populated parts of Spain.

Source : Abbey National Offshore Survey

and hang gliding. Football, rugby, running and hockey are now passive, watching sports as the battle with the waistline is probably lost. Similarly a short cycle ride to the supermarket seems to be more appropriate than dressing up each Sunday in bright lycra matching outfits, ripping calf muscles to shreds, ascending narrow mountain roads astride the latest 21-gear machine.

No! It is time to put the more active stuff on the back burner. Slow down. Remember, this is Spain – where time is not important. Consider the less athletic pursuits where skill, knowledge and abilities can be honed to perfection with practice, practice and more practice. Golf and bowls perhaps. Tennis, or hiking. Tone up at a gym. Take up fishing.

Golf

Golf in Spain is booming, driven by tourism and the climate. The world wide success of Ballesteros, Olazabal, Jimenez and Garcia have contributed to this success. Ballesteros is a star in Spain, an icon in Britain and if he had been Italian would by now have been immortalised on the ceiling of the Sistine Chapel.

The Costa Del Sol is often referred to as Costa Del Golf, such is the profusion of new courses. They are carved out of barren landscapes, pampered and watered to produce lush green fairways. Consequently golf is not cheap: 45 Euros for a round is common. In Scotland, the home of golf, it is a game for the working man. In Spain it is a game for the tourist and the wealthy resident.

The pursuit of golf always necessitates a visit to the local golf shop where the latest technology, graphite shafted, titanium headed, clubs can be purchased which are designed to forgive the advancing years but not a bank balance. High prices and a limited choice suggests this visit is best made outside Spain.

Bowling

The capital cost to establish a bowling green is low. Demand is high. It is one of the few competitive sports for those of advancing years which combines well with social activities. Such is its popularity on the Costa Blanca that a winter league of nine clubs has a full page devoted to its activities in the local weekly paper.

Hiking

Walking or hiking clubs exist in all the main areas. For the adventuresome, the best places to go are the Picos De Europe in northern Spain, the Pyrenees near the French border, the Costa Blanca inland from Benidorm and around the Sierra Nevada. Strangely, hiking is not too popular with Spaniards but is hugely popular with new foreign residents.

Many holiday companies offer Spanish walking tours. This has given rise to some excellent English language publications describing good detailed routes with clear concise maps. The trails themselves are way-marked, the only hazards being dogs and the unhygienic nature of some refuge huts. It is important not to underestimate some of these trails with rapidly changing weather, snow on high ground and exposure on steep paths.

Fishing

Spaniards fish, dipping their line into the clear blue Mediterranean from pier, boat or shore. They can even keep several rods going at the same time. So popular is fishing that the basic equipment is sold in supermarkets or newspaper shops. Sea fishing from the shore is still a sport for the youngster with only the smaller species being caught. River or lake fishing in northern Spain is a far more serious matter altogether, with trout and salmon, pike and carp available. The local tourist office is the place to enquire about licences, season tickets and such like.

Tennis

Tennis is a low capital cost, highly popular activity. The courts, many of which are attached to hotels or sports centres, are utilised all year around. Many urbanisations, in addition to a swimming pool, have a tennis court maintained through their community charge. It can be a social activity too. This choice is dependent on the membership or the availability of a teaching professional.

Running

It is not too hot to run! Spain, like all countries, has its runners and joggers. It has superstars too. It has often been host to international athletics meetings. Each town has its own sports ground complete with a running track. Marathons and half marathons are commonplace – but not in summer.

Gyms

Many privately run gymnasiums tend to be devoted to muscle building. northern Europeans much prefer the weight reduction clubs of bright lycra, cardio-vascular training, running and cycling machines, sauna and steam bath. Modern gymnasiums exist, many located in new building complexes.

Sports federations

There are many other sports available – squash, skiing in the Sierra Nevada, beach and water sports, horse riding, mountaineering, gliding, cycling, and of course football, football and more football. Each sport has its own federation, which is always a good starting point for information.

JOINING A SOCIAL CLUB

El tiempo libre does not just mean sport, it means free time.
   Social clubs are in abundance as ex-pats of similar nationalities

bond together around a common interest. In the *Costa Blanca News* there are hundreds of English-speaking social clubs advertised weekly. You name it and it exists. Traditional clubs such the Buffaloes, the Labour Club, the Conservative Club, the Bridge Club, and the Solo Club. Many dancing clubs too such as line dancing, Scottish dancing, sequence dancing, Spanish dancing and Yellow Rock Square dancing. Active clubs such as the computer club, the Barber Shop Singers, the Gilbert and Sullivan Society, walking and running clubs also compete for one's interest.

Social clubs are a method of meeting people, of sharing a common interest, past or present. It is a meeting place to deal with problems, or to seek information. They are an aid to settling in a new country. Golf and bowls may be the top sports, but a meal, a drink or a visit to the club are the main social activities.

SUMMARY

- Motoring in the wide open country is still a pleasure. Fuel is cheap. Popular cars are Ford and Seat.

- The postal system is identified by the colour yellow. It is satisfactory at its best but has nothing to commend it.

- Names and addresses are unusual. It is important to get them correct.

- Television is now digital. It is possible to receive English TV, radio and daily newspapers.

- There are three police forces.

- Foreigners do not party like the Spanish, preferring to keep to their own national groups.

- Spain is a wonderful country for sporting activities. Golf, bowls, hiking and tennis are the most popular.

- One unusual feature of life abroad for the ex-pat is the profusion of social clubs.

16

Avoiding Failure

A NEED TO LEARN

This book is about success. Success in realising a goal. Success in achieving a dream. For some people, no matter how hard they try, life in Spain is not for them. Whatever the reason they return home saddened by the experience. We need to learn from these situations.

A property bought on a whim, the difficulty of visualising a home from a plan or drawing, high pressure selling, financial problems or difficulty in absorbing the Spanish culture may be reasons for rejecting life in a new country. Fortunately these failures are few and far between, for if there is a will to do so, these problems can be overcome.

The true explanation for people going back home probably lies elsewhere.

CASE STUDY : EMPLOYMENT

It had been an excellent night out. Local singers had put on fantastic, popular entertainment of a high professional standard. We followed it up with a good meal and some wine. At around 2.00 am last drinks were taken in a Spanish bar.

An English couple, in their late 30s or early 40s, were sitting on their own. They looked forlorn. We asked them to join us for 'one more'. It transpired this was their last week-end in Spain. They had sold their property and were returning home.

They were curious to know why we liked Spain so much. We too were curious to know what had gone wrong with their attempts to build a new life. Apparently they had come to Spain to work and live but after three years had not been able to obtain suitable employment. Neither could speak Spanish.

We listened sympathetically. Not a lot could be done at this late stage. No point in giving advice when a decision had been made and implemented. Yet the solution was blindingly obvious. Learn Spanish!

If you want a good career in Spain it is absolutely essential that you speak the language. If not, the only employment available is working in an English-speaking bar or restaurant or setting up your own business servicing English-speaking clients.

REASONS FOR FAILURE

Holiday homes

The purchase of a holiday home is normally financially sound when property inflation is taken into account. Inflation, however, is not cash flow and the annual outlay for flights, running costs and taxes all mount up, and may be more than a budget allows.

A permanent holiday home is also great, but using it to a maximum constrains holidaying elsewhere.

Women residents

Women permanent residents find it harder to settle in Spain than their men folk. Family and grandchildren can be missed. While this wrench can be minimised by holidays, the physiological barrier of time and distance is still an obstacle.

Dusty, windswept building sites do not aid the settling in process.

In southern Spain the phenomenon of 'Sahara rain' occurs

once or twice per year. Rain clouds moving north from the
Sahara desert deposit a thick red dust on new clean white
houses. This disconcerting act of nature necessitates a major
clean up with brushes, water and power hoses. It can be
discouraging.

Retirement

At the end of a long working life retirement is a goal richly
deserved. But it can be hard to stand back and relax. The cut and
thrust of business can be missed, particularly when
entrepreneurial opportunities in Spain are clearly obvious.
People may have been married for 40 years, but living in each
other's company for 24 hours per day, 7 days per week is a new
experience. Tensions can develop. Some people go back to
work. Some people go back home.

Nothing to do

Boredom can be a killer. After the house is sorted, the car
running smoothly and the garden done, what do we do next? It
is important to keep an active mind and body for the soporific
heat of the Spanish sun will soon slow the senses. Sun
worshipping, the daily gin and tonic or serious *cerveza* (beer)
drinking can make for an easy life, but only in the short term.

Tolerance

A more complex reason exists for people returning home. It has
nothing to do with bricks and mortar, nothing to do with the
physical aspects of change, nothing to do with Spain. It is about
human relationships. Back home, people have spent 40 or so
years achieving their position in a class-divided society,
represented on one level by their place of residence. The
detached house in Oslo, the apartment in Dublin, the block in
Frankfurt, the cottage in Antwerp, the terraced row in Burnley

are all forgotten and replaced by a single status society 'of what you are now and not what you were'. Since equality on the urbanisation is the name of the game, it is hardly surprising tensions occur.

Naturally primary groups form. The golf fanatics, the night owls, the heavy drinkers, the restaurant dwellers, or simply those who wish to gossip. Others may want to keep to themselves. Either way they may get on with each other, or they may not. Tolerance is needed. Tolerance to accept different life styles, different needs, different backgrounds.

But tolerance is rarely given because its need is seldom understood.

SUMMARY

- We need to learn why people go back home.

- To work professionally in Spain it is necessary to learn the language.

- Women find it hard to settle. They miss their offspring, family and friends. They have to contend with dusty building sites and Sahara rain.

- There is a need to keep the body and mind active. Boredom is a killer.

- Tolerance of other people is required on an urbanisation.

Appendix 1
A Purchase Contract issued by a builder for a new property

Place .... Date ....

Parties

On the one part is the Vendor ....
registered with number .... living at
.... represented with power of attorney by
.... with NIE number ....

On the other part, as Purchaser(s) ....
with UK Nationality and .... with UK
Nationality living at ....
with passport numbers respectively of ....
and................................

Both parties consider each other to have sufficient legal power to enter into this purchase and sale contract by mutual agreement.

Statements

One: .... is the sole owner of a plot of land situated inside the Plan Parcial .... with number .... in the municipal district of .... It was acquired by virtue of private contract signed with .... The plot is free of loans and charges. The deeds of the planned urbanisation has been registered at the Registry Office of ....
It was signed on .... before the Notary
....

193

Two: On the above mentioned area will be built 458 bungalows as per plans and drawings prepared by Master Architect .... living at .... The builder is .... living at .... who reserves the right to modify the number of bungalows or apartments or the project itself, if necessary, due to architectural or town planning reasons.

Any modification of the project for technical or legal reasons will be agreed by the Town Hall or the architect, or the master builder.

Three: That among the bungalows or apartments is number .... in the urbanisation of .... with a usable surface of approximately 64.00 square metres, a built one of 76.00 square metres and a plot size of approximately 100.00 square metres consisting of the following elements:

A DUPLEX WITH THREE BEDROOMS, DINING-SITTING ROOM, KITCHEN, BATHROOM, TOILET, TERRACE AND SOLARIUM.

Four: The Vendor .... is interested in selling the described property and the Purchaser .... in buying it, according to the following clauses:

Clauses

FIRST: .... sells to .... who buys the property described in the third statement of this contract.

The selling is carried out with all rights, facilities and services which are inherent in the sold property, the results of the building project and the development rules including the proportionate part, corresponding to the communal element zones of the urbanisation.

In the sale are included all the communal rights of the urbanisation called .... The maintenance of the communal area is paid by the owners for the present and future phases.

SECOND: The total agreed purchase price of the property amounts to .... Euros plus the corresponding Value Added Tax (IVA). This sum will be paid as follows:

* When the purchaser signs the contract he will pay the amount of .... Euros in cash.

* On .... the purchaser will pay the amount of .... Euros with a cheque made out to ....

* On .... the purchaser will pay the amount of .... Euros with a cheque made out to ....

* The balance of the total price will be paid by the purchaser when he signs the *escritura* plus 7% IVA.

THIRD: .... will deliver the property described in the third statement of this contract in the Month of .... approximately.

FOURTH: The date of delivery of the property will be notified to the Purchaser by the Vendor the moment the property is finished and in a correct condition to be used and at this date the Purchaser will take charge of all communal expenses of the urbanisation and any other costs which may be derived from the maintenance of the communal aspects of the urbanisation.

FIFTH: In the event the Purchaser is not able to pay the amount of one or more of the payments on the established date, which is indicated in the second clause of the contract, and notifies the Vendor in writing, the Purchaser can pay the balance with corresponding interest.

As compensation for non fulfilment of the Contract, the Vendor will keep 50% of each paid sum that the Purchaser should have made to the date on which Vendor decides to resolve the contract.

SIXTH: Upon the agreed price being paid in full, plus cost of the applicable taxes and other agreed obligations, the Vendor will grant to the Purchaser the *escritura* to be issued before the Notary nominated by the former, in the city of
.... within in a period of fifteen days from the date of payment.

SEVENTH: The Purchaser undertakes to respect and follow the obligations established in the statutes of the urbanisation to which the described property belongs, authorising the Vendor to constitute the Community of Owners, which will follow the Initial Statutes and approve new Statutes together with all the co-owners according to the Horizontal Property Law. Likewise the Purchaser authorises the Vendor to contract water and electricity on his behalf. Until the Community of Owners is formed the Vendor is authorised to take the necessary measures for the correct administration of the community.

EIGHTH: All extra expenses derived from the purchase of the property (water and electricity connection, Notary and Registry, documented juridical acts, etc.) will be paid by the Purchaser, who authorises the Vendor to draw up water and electricity contracts. After the date of delivery of the property the Purchaser will take care of all the water and electricity expenses incurred by the property. If on completion the electrical company Iberdrola has not made the connection for the electrical meters, the Purchaser promises to send to the Vendor receipts for consumption. When completed the Purchaser will pay a deposit of .... Euros representing costs for the next few months. When the meters are fitted the Vendor will adjust the payments. If the Purchaser has paid too much the Vendor will return the balance and on the contrary if the Purchaser has paid too little, he will pay the difference to the Vendor.

NINTH: IVA (Value Added Tax) will be set according to Spanish legislation.

TENTH: For any legal matter between the Vendor and Purchaser as notified at the heading of this contract, where the Purchaser is a non-resident, it will be submitted to his legal address.

ELEVENTH: The property is exclusively allowed to be used as a dwelling house.

TWELFTH: In the event of any dispute arising from this contract, the parties submit themselves expressly to the Courts and Tribunals of .... and their superiors, or by default the Courts and Tribunals of .... renouncing any others to which they might otherwise be entitled, as this document shall be governed according to the Laws in Spain.

THIRTEENTH: The Vendor guarantees the strict fulfilment of everything stated in this Contract and is not obliged to do anything which is not written in the Contract.

FOURTEENTH: Furniture, curtains, lamps, covers, mirrors, electric units or any ornamental units are not included in the sale price of the property.

FIFTEENTH: It is obligatory for all foreigners in Spain to have a fiscal number (N.I.E.) (Spanish Legislation, Decree of 2 February 1996, Article 61).

Both contracting parties hereof being in conformity and agreement with the above, sign this Purchase Contract in duplicate in the place and on the date first before written:

The Vendor   (signature)   The Purchaser   (signature)

Appendix 2
The community rules

The aim of the following STATUTES is to stipulate rules
owners must observe in order to ensure the best functioning of
the Urbanisation and the maintenance of relationships between
neighbours.

All those deeds which have not been included in the
STATUTES OF THE COMMUNITY OWNERS are to be
resolved according to the HORIZONTAL PROPERTY LAW
49/1960 AND POSTERIOR REFORM BY LAW 8/1.999,
published on 8 April 1999.

The Property

1. The *Escritura* describes the services and facilities of each
property. Therefore, according to the Law 8/1.999, chapter 11,
Art. 7, each property owner can modify the architectural
elements, facilities or services of the property provided the
security of the building, exterior appearance, general structure
or shape is not changed or diminished, and the rights of other
owners are not prejudiced.

2. The owners or occupants of the property are not allowed to
carry on activities which are forbidden in these statutes, harm
the building or infringe general laws with bothersome,
unhealthy, dangerous or illegal activities.

3. All owners are under the following obligations:-
   a. When using the facilities of the Community and other
   communal elements, whether they are for general or private
   use, to make good and avoid any damage.
   b. To keep the house and garden tidy.

c. The house is to be used exclusively for residential purposes.

d. The grilles, walls, awnings and all the external elements must follow a model approved by the Community.

e. To contribute to the general expenses of the Community proportionate to the amount which appears in each *Escritura*, the final date for payment being one month from date of invoice.

f. To communicate to the Secretary-Administrator of the Community an address in Spain to receive receipt of notification and summons from the Community. In the absence of this communication, the address will be taken as the owner's property in the Urbanisation. The notifications handed to the occupants will take judicial effect.

g. According to the previous paragraph, if it was impossible to issue a notification or summons addressed to an owner, it is understood that it will be placed on the Community notice board or on other visible place of general use, signed by the Secretary-Administrator and with the approval of the President. A notification made by this means will have the full judical effect.

h. To keep silent during the rest time, from 14.00 to 16.00 hours in the afternoon and after 24.000 hours.

i. Rubbish and gardening waste are to be deposited in the rubbish containers, by means of well-closed plastic bags.

j. Repairs and any other building works which have been authorised by the Community, do not imply the right to obstruct the pavements and/or road with building material, except for cases in which it be necessary. In these cases the materials are to be deposited in as little space as possible, keeping the area clear for pedestrians and vehicles. When the works are finished the owner is obliged to clean the area leaving the pavements and road in a perfect condition.

k. All domestic animals must be accompanied by their owners and leashed when out of doors. Furthermore, the owner will not allow domestic animals to relieve themselves in the Urbanisation, and if this happens the owner will pick up the excrement.

Community Board

4. The managerial posts of the Community are as follows:
    4.1   President
    4.2   Vice-President
    4.3   Secretary
    4.4   Administrator
    4.5   Board Members

All the managerial posts are elected for one year. All those designated can be removed from their post before the expiration of the period by agreement at an Extraordinary Meeting of Property Owners.

5. The President is to be designated from among the owners by election or draw. The designation is to be compulsory, although the owner designated can demand his relief to a Judge one month after his election, giving due reason. The Community will consult with a Judge when the Meeting could not appoint a President of the Community.

The President is to hold the legal representation of the Community in all matters concerning the Community.

The length of the appointment is one year. It is possible to re-elect the President at the Ordinary General Meeting by majority of those owners present. In this case, the President is allowed to refuse the post without the need to state a reason.

5.1 The President is to have a mobile telephone.

5.2 The General Meeting is to approve a cash turnover of 1200 Euros /year. The President is to have available this amount for small repairs, works or improvements, without having to consult the General Meeting and justifying this expense by means of corresponding invoices.

5.3 All those works, repairs or improvements which exceed the amount allocated to the President are to be agreed by the General Meeting, from at least three different estimates.

6. The Vice-President is to take responsibility for standing in for the President in his absence or inability, as well as to assist him in his work according to the terms established by General Meeting.

7. The duties of Secretary and Administrator are to be carried out by the President, unless the hiring of a Collegiate Administrator by means of the present statues is agreed (Chapter 11, Art. 13, Paragraph 5, Law 8/1.000).

Communal Areas

8. The floor, projections, foundations, party walls and other elements described in the article 396 of the Civil Code and Law 49/1.960 of 21 July are communal elements. So to are the inside streets of the Community, garden, swimming pools, TV and FM installations, lighting, toilets and other facilities.

9. It is not allowed to make any modification, work or repair to the referred communal elements if it is has not been approved by the General Meeting of the Community, who would request a technical feasibility report and the pertinent licences.

10. No owner can claim the right to a parking space in his garden, since in no title deed is it stated the garden should have access for vehicles or inside parking. If the property has a vehicle entry in the garden it will depend on the goodwill of the neighbours to keep this access clear. Bulky vehicles, trucks, big vans, and machinery cannot be parked in the private streets of the Urbanisation. The vehicles parked in private streets must be moved to the other side of the street every fifteen days, in order to clean the streets. All those vehicles parked in the private streets for more than two months are to be removed to a nearby place. In this case the crane hired to remove the vehicle is to be paid by the owner.

11. All owners must observe the Statutes, informing the President of any infringement, in order to take any necessary measures according to the seriousness of the infringement or damage caused.

Use of Swimming Pools

12. The swimming pools, as communal areas, are at the disposal of all owners, who must respect them at all times.

13. According to the Decree 25511997 of 7 December, by the Valencia Government, which regulates the Hygienic-Sanitary and Security rules for swimming pools, Art. 2, the area made up of the vessel or vessels and the surrounding area destined for bath or swimming, as well as the installations and facilities necessary to ensure the perfect functioning and performance of the recreational activity, are to be defined as the swimming pool.

14. The two swimming pools belonging to the Urbanisation are catalogued as private swimming pools, since they do not have more than 200 m2 of water lamina (surface).

15. The swimming timetable is to be from 10.00 to 21.00 hours, during the summer months, the entry controlled by means of swipe cards issued by the Administrator and with the approval of the President. For the remainder of the year only the second swimming pool is to be open.

16. Since both swimming pools are defined as private, it is not necessary to hire lifeguards and therefore the Community declines any responsibility for accidents inside the facilities, except in the case of those covered by the insurance policy taken out by the Community.

17. During the months of July and August two caretakers are to be hired, one for each swimming pool. The caretakers are to have the following tasks:

   a) Working timetable: from 9.30 to 14.30 hours and from 16.30 to 21.00 hours

   b) To clean and remove the rubbish from the swimming pool area, to disinfect the floor of the showers and if necessary to clean the bottom of the pool.

   c) To check the performance of all facilities, writing down any shortcomings, flaws or damages in a daybook.

   d) To check the water condition at the beginning of the

day and write down the analytical parametres of pH and mg/1 of disinfectant.
e) To control the entry of users, by requesting the presentation of an updated card and denying admission to those owners and guests whose names appear on a black list provided by the Administrator.
f) To ensure the application of hygiene and security rules, avoiding personal confrontation at all times.
g) To facilitate access for disabled people and ensure that they have seating.
h) In case of an emergency or injury, the caretaker will call telephone number 112 urgently.

18. Children under 9 years are to be accompanied by their parents or guardians.

19. The use of flippers, playing with balls, and swimming without clothes, is not allowed.

20. It is also strictly forbidden to enter with animals, to bring bottles and glasses inside the swimming pool precinct, or to eat or drink, except snacks, in which case the tins, cartons and rubbish must be deposited in the rubbish bin.

21. Chairs, parasols, air mattresses and floats for adults are not allowed in the swimming pool.

22. Solar creams must be eliminated before going into the water by means of a shower.

23. Everyone, without exception, must have a shower before going into the water.

Appendix 3
The escritura

A DEED OF PURCHASE AND SALE

Protocol Number ....

In .... (name of town) my place of
residence, on .... (date) Before me,
.... (full name), Notario of this City
and of the Illustrious College of Valencia

APPEARS

Representing the party selling
.... (full name), of age, married,
inhabitant of this city, with address in ....
.... (full address) and with DNI number ....
....

And the party buying ....

Mr .... (full name) of British
nationality, of age, divorced, living in ....
.... (full address) and with Passport Number
....

He accredits his nationality with the document of identification
before quoted but does not accredit his NIE and he is advised by
me, the Notary, that according to R.D. of February 2 1996 in
Article 61, it is obligatory for foreigners in Spain to have a
Foreigners Identity Number.

He confirms that he is Non-Resident and that the investment
is not from offshore funds and is legal according to the RD
664/00 of April 23.

REPRESENTATION

.... (full name) in representation with
Power of Attorney for .... (building
company full name) formed for an indefinite time on the
.... (date) before the Notario of
.... (name of City),
.... (name of Notario) with the
number of his Protocol .... with official
C.I.F. number .... and office address
....

The object of the company is to promote, construct and sell
for themselves or for others, all types of buildings with related
operations, such as the purchase of land, urbanisation,
parcelling, letting, and administration.

THEY STATE

.... (name of company) has
complete and official power over the following housing
urbanisation under construction.

Description
Within the boundaries of .... (name of
town), Plan .... the second phase of
project ...., a house with two floors
joined by means of an internal stairway. This one is marked
commercially with the number .... Looking at the façade from
the east this is the eighth of its type and there exist eight running
from right to left. There is independent access through the
garden. There are surfaces built, closed and indoors of seventy
six square metres and sixty four useful square metres, twelve
metres distributed in terraces, various departments, rooms and
services. Looking at the front, at the right is the house with
commercial number..... and its garden, left the street. Adjoining
the bottom is a chalet with commercial number .... and its
garden.

Community Quota

The property is assigned a quota of the common elements, benefits and charges in relation to a total value of 0.67%.

Inscription

The property is Inscribed in the Property Register of
.... (town) book 1357, volume 1122, folio 13, property 23456, first inscription.

Local Tax Contribution

Those appearing declare the lack of the tax receipt because it is still to be issued, which I have duly noted.

Title

Acquired for purchase by the commercial organisation
.... (name of company purchasing the land) stated in the deed granted on the ....
(date) before the Notary of .... (town),
.... (name), number ....
of his Protocol.

The new work and horizontal division is declared, before the Notary of .... (town)
.... (name) the day .... (date)

Origin

The house described forms part of the second phase of the group 'Al Andalus' comprising two phases; the first phase comprising 274 dwellings and the second phase 184 dwellings. The second phase of the group urbanisation called 'Al Andalus', in the boundaries of Orihuela, in the urbanisation Partial Plan 'Las Piscinas' is composed of this residencial group of 184 dwellings, of which 62 are ground floor, 62 are first floor denominated bungalows and 60 individual, denominated chalets.

It is built on the plot of land 73 (parcela EH.4.4), in the boundaries of Orihuela, belonging to the Part Plan 'Las Piscinas', Sector J-1, with a superficial extension of 19.668 metres square dedicated to high residential construction. North is the limit of the part plan, south the road, east Parcel EH.2.1, and west, parcel EH.2.3

Charges

It is free of them, except for any fiscal obligations of the tenants and lessees and the current payment of the quotas to the community declared by the sellers. The buyer accepts the Certificate sent by the Secretary, previously approved by the President.

The plot on which the properties are located is liable to the costs of urbanisation, in conformity with Article 178 of the Regulation of Administration of Urbanisations which has been endorsed by the sellers.

Information Registry

The Notary makes known that the description of the property, its ownership and the charges, in the form previously referred to, are of the statements of the sellers, of the title of property shown to me and of the Nota Simple of the registration of the property, obtained by me, which I have seen.

Regarding the deed of new work and horizontal division mentioned in the title, which I have seen, I write the following : Common Elements and the Law of Horizontal Property are the results of the application of Article 396 of the Civil Code and Law 49/1.960 of 21 July with the following:

1. The common elements are the floors, stairs, foundations, wall supports and party walls, facades, patios and other that determines Article 396 of the Civil Code, and the services of combined use, not already referred to or included among the common elements.

2. The owners of the different elements finance their expenses and enjoy the rights of the common elements in the proportion marked by their corresponding quotas. Therefore the expenses of maintenance services, cleaning, surveillance, illumination etc. that are used by all, will be distributed amongst all, using the previously established quota.

3. The administration of the common elements is commended to a Meeting of Owners, composed of a President, Secretary and others that are named. Until such a meeting is constituted the administration will provisionally be conferred to a person or

company named by the developer who undertakes the administration of this Urbanisation, even naming the corresponding administrators, being the honorarium of those in charge of other communities to fix the quotas to be paid by the owners conforming to the above number 2.

4. The apartments, no matter how many times the owners request it, will not be the subject of regrouping, aggregation, segregation, division or subdivision, and in general any other modification, except for reasonable access as appropriate for opening new holes to common elements.

5. The area of recreation and swimming pool is designated inside the group green areas of size about a thousand square metres. It will not only be used by the holders of the described dwellings, but also by the owners of the dwellings of the already declared phase 1 in the adjacent parcel that constitutes the group. Together with phase 1, this will finance the expenses of the use of the green areas, pool and recreation, in proportion to the useful surface of the dwellings.

6. The walls that separate the different elements of the group will be built following the pattern approved by the constructor with the object of uniformity within the Urbanisation. No modifications, or the use of ornamental materials can be undertaken without the constructor's previous consent.

7. The owners of the dwellings cannot cover the existing air vents located under the dwelling for ventilation.

8. The owners of the dwellings on the top floor, who enjoy the use of their terraces, are responsible for the cleaning of the existing drains, it being their responsibility and not that of the constructor for smells and dampness.

9. The constructor reserves the right to put in the deed any modification, explanation, or rectification that is necessary for the good of the Urbanisation provided such modifications do not alter the quotas of the elements already notified. The constructor reserves the right to alter the construction of certain elements in different ways to the ones declared in this deed.

The commercial representative reserves the right to conduct, to constitute and to give rights, real or personal, to supply companies such as Iberdrola, Aquagest, Telefonica, or any other that is appropriate.

THEY GRANT

First The company .... as it is represented, sells the property described previously, free of obligations, as well as current taxes, with all its uses, rights and servitudes, to .... (name) who buys it.

Second The agreed price is .... Euros (price in figures and words). The seller declares having already received part of the purchase price from the buyer who completes the transaction with a bank draft.

Third As is conventional to the contracting parties, all expenses to the making of this deed will be paid by the buyer including the Municipal Tax on the Increment of the Value of Lands.

Fourth The seller to receive from the buyer the Value Added Tax (IVA) that is to say 7% on the conventional price as entered in the Treasury publication.

Fifth The buyer agrees to accept the norms of the community and to have received a letter with a recommendation on maintenance from .... (name of the community administrator of properties).

Sixth The buyer recognises that, by virtue of this sale, he assumes responsibility for the payment of electricity and water, and any other bills relevant to the house as well as carrying out any appropriate maintenance.

Seventh It is understood that the seller of the dwelling has given to the buyer a multi risk buildings insurance policy taken out with .... for one year.

Eighth The buyer names as his fiscal representative
.... (name)
.... (address)

They say this and they grant

I give them advice, legal and fiscal warnings, especially those with regard to the thirty working days for the authorisation of this deed, to liquidate the same, and to effect the Tax on *Patrimonia Transmissions* and *Documented Juridical Acts*, as well as being affected by the consequence of this Tax and the present document. I read this deed which is verbally translated into English for the convenience of the buyer, the translator being known by me, by name of .... with residence in .... and with residence card number ....

I give again the warning made previously by me, the Notary, that the buyer had the right to an official translator but this was not required and finding that the document is satisfactory they sign, in the presence of the translator, with me the Notary, and that I publish the deed in 9 legal pages of the series 3s, numbers 456789 to 8 numbers in sequence.

I GIVE FAITH

The signatures of those appearing are
.... (representative of the seller with Power of Attorney)
.... (buyer)
.... (notary)
.... (translator)

Appendix 4
A purchase contract drawn up by an *Abogado*

THE CONTRATO PRIVADO DE COMPRAVENTA
(Full Private Contract)

At .... (address) on .... (date)

GATHERED

On the one part,
The spouses Mr .... and Mrs ...., of age
.............., living at .... (address) with D.N.I.
numbers 44.55.66 y 23.24.25 respectively.
And the other,
Mr .... and Mrs ...., of age ...., living
at .... (address) with current Residencia numbers
56.57.58. and 43.45.46 respectively.
All present are in their own names and rights and are recognised
to have the capacity to complete the private contract of sale and
purchase.

THEY STATE

That the spouses Mr .... and Mrs .... are
the rightful owners of the following property:
    Urban dwelling, in a state of ruin, situated in ....
(full address): comprising ground floor with room and coral,
occupying forty square metres.
    Adjoining property: Looking from the street, right entrance
belongs to the heirs of Mr ...., the left entrance

belong to the heirs of Mr ...., the land at the back belongs to the Hermitage of the Calvary, and in front of the dwelling is the street.

It is inscribed in the Property Register of .... (town) in volume 1212, book 43, folio 12, house reference number 2.345.

CHARGES ON THE PROPERTY: MORTGAGE IN FAVOUR OF .... (BANK)

For twenty seven thousand and forty five euros for two years with ordinary interest of 11.5%, and for three years delay interest of 17.5% on 540 euros for costs. Commenced 3.03.1996. Formalised in deed on 13.03.1996 and authorised by the Notary of .... (town) .... (name).

TITLE

The property belongs to the spouses Mr .... and Mrs .... for the purchase made for the children Mr .... and Mrs .... by virtue of a purchase and sale *Escritura* authorised by the Notary Mr .... of .... (town) on 02.09.87 with reference number 745.

CLAUSES

FIRST: That by virtue of the present contract the spouses Mr .... and Mrs .... commit to sell, and Mr .... and Mrs .... commit to buy, the property previously described together with the rights that are inherent. The property is sold free of charges, encumbrances, mortgages or any other limitations that affect the rights. The sellers commit to carry out whatever operations are necessary to arrive at the date specified with a property in a completely free state and stated correctly in the *Escritura*.

SECOND: The total price of the sale and purchase is
.... Euros.

A) Form of payment: the buyers pay to the sellers a deposit of
.... Euros as part payment of the agreed total sum.

B) The remaining sum of the total price of the sale and
purchase .... Euros will be paid by the buyers at the
moment of the signing of the corresponding *Escritura*.

C)The signing of the corresponding public *Escritura* will be
before .... (date).

THIRD: The expenses that are derived from completing the
Escritura will be to the account of the buyer with the exception
of the plus valia which will be to the account of the seller. Also
to the account of the seller will be all the charges derived from
the cancellation of the mortgages as well as those for the work
of amplification of the *Escritura*.

FOURTH: If the buyer, for reasons unaware to the seller, seeks
to resolve the contract in an unilateral way, it is understood that
the buyer will forfeit to the seller the amount already paid. In
the case that the seller defaults double the amount will be
returned to the buyer.

Failure to pay the balance of the price, ... Euros by
the date .... will result in the resolution of this
contract coming into effect.

FIFTH: The contracting parties agree that any questions or
problems that could be raised by reason of this contract are to be
made expressly to the Tribunals of ....

SIXTH: Both parties designate the address given at the heading
of this document in order to effect notifications, requirements,
and citations.

**The sellers and the buyers sign this present contract in
duplicate in the place and date established in the heading.**

Signature Sellers　　　　　　　　　**Signature Buyers**

Appendix 5
An Option Contract signed on behalf of a client by an agent

.... and ....
with Irish passports numbers ....
and .... respectively, living at
.... (henceforth, the Buyers)

are interested in purchasing the following property:

Number .... in Residencial ....
Urbanisation ....
This property is sold to them by the Agent ....
.... with C.I.F. number ....
in representation of .... a UK
citizen, resident in this property (henceforth, the Seller), and
with the following N.I.E. number ....

under the following stipulations:

First. The agreed price is ....
Euros. The purchase includes furniture, full kitchen appliances
and items according to the attached list.

Second. On signing this contract, the Buyers pay a reservation
deposit of .... Euros to the Agent
.... the present contract serving as a
receipt thereof. If the Buyers should breach any of the
agreements established herein, they will lose the deposit. If the
Seller should become in breach of this agreement, the Buyers
are entitled to receive the deposit in double.

Third. The Buyers accept to pay the remaining part of the total price .... Euros at the signing of the Title Deed, which will take place no later than ....

Fourth. The Seller has the obligation to pay and cancel any debts, encumbrances, limitations or prohibitions that the property may have inscribed at the Land Registry.

Fifth. All fees and taxes related to this agreement and to the Title Deed until its inscription at the Land Registry are included in the above price, except the Plus Valia Tax which is the obligation of the Seller.

Sixth. Any discrepancies that may arise between the parties with regard to the present agreement shall be resolved at the Law Courts of .... according to Spanish Law.

Signed in .... on ....

The Buyers   The Seller **(Agent)**

Appendix 6
The communities of Spain and their Provinces

The provinces of Spain are grouped into 17 autonomous Communities and two autonomous cities in north Africa. The provincial numbers appear as the first two digits in postcodes.

Northern Spain

Galicia

15	A Coruna
27	Lugo
32	Ourense
36	Pontevedra

Asturias, Cantabria

33	Asturias
39	Cantabria

Basque, Navarra, La Rioja

01	Alava
20	Guipuzcoa
48	Vizcaya
31	Navarra
26	La Rioja

Eastern Spain

Catalonia

08	Barcelona
25	Lleida
17	Girona
43	Tarragona

Aragon

	22	Huesca
	44	Teruel
	50	Zaragoza

Valencia, Murcia

	03	Alicante
	46	Valencia
	12	Castellon
	30	Murcia

Central Spain

Madrid

	28	Communidad de Madrid

Castilla la Mancha

	02	Albacete
	13	Ciudad Real
	16	Cuenca
	19	Guadalajara
	45	Toledo

Extremadura

	06	Babajoz
	10	Caceres

Castilla y Leon

	05	Avila
	09	Burgos
	24	Leon
	34	Palencia
	37	Salamanca
	40	Segovia
	42	Soria
	47	Valladolid
	49	Zamora

Southern Spain

Andalucia

	04	Almeria

11	Cadiz
14	Cordoba
18	Granada
21	Huelva
23	Jaen
29	Malaga
41	Sevilla

Islands

Balearic Islands

| 07 | Baleares |

Canary Islands

| 35 | Las Palmas |
| 37 | Santa Cruz de Tenerife |

Appendix 7
Public holidays

1 January	New Years Day
6 January	Kings Day
19 March	St Joseph's Day
March/April	Good Friday or Easter Sunday
1 May	Labour Day
25 July	St James Day
15 August	Assumption of the Virgin
12 October	National Day
1 November	All Saints Day
6 December	Constitution Day
8 December	Immaculate Conception
25 December	Christmas Day

The central government allows 14 days paid public holidays per year: 12 of these days are highlighted. Additionally each region celebrates its own holiday with most towns and villages also having their own carnival and fiesta days. If a holiday falls on a Tuesday or Thursday, shops and offices may be closed on the intervening Monday or Friday, making it a long weekend.

Northern Europeans find the frequency of Spanish holidays confusing, ignoring all but the main religious holidays.

Appendix 8
English language newspapers

Costa Blanca News	Apartado 95, 03500 Benidorm
Costa del Sol News	Apartado 102, 29630 Benalmadena Costa (Malaga)
Sur in English	Avda Doctor Maranon 48, 29009 Malaga
The Mallorca Daily Bulletin	San Filiu 25, Palma
The Island Gazette	Calle Iriarte 43, Santa Cruz, Tenerife

Appendix 9
Useful addresses

New property

Atlas International	83 South St, Dorking, Surrey.
Masa International UK	Airport House, Purley House, Croydon.
Propertunities Ltd	13/17 Newbury St, Wantage, Oxon.
Grupo Fin	69 Tidings Hill, Haltstead, Essex CO9 1BJ.
Spain Direct	22 Poole Hill, Bournemouth, Dorset.

Property websites

Taylor Woodrow	www.taywoodspain.co.uk
Spanish property portal	www.newhabitat.com
Spanish private sales	www.loot.com

Timeshare

Residence Condominium International	www.rci.co.uk
Keyworld	www.keyworldinvest.com
Guide to Timeshares	www.guidetotimeshare.com

Holiday homes

Parador Rentals	Cabo Roig, 03189 Orihuela Costa, Alicante
Internet site	www.europropertysearch.com
Internet site	www.holidayhome.co.uk

Interpreting

Susana Bulitude	Calle Principal de Asturias 9, 03700 Javea
Simply Translating	www.lshl.com

Financial planning

Blevins and Franks	Barbican House, 26/34 Old Street, London EC1V 9QQ
Henry Woods	Calle Azorin 4, 29600 Marbella
Towry Law Financial Solutions Ltd	42/46 Greyfriars Road, Reading RG1 1NN

Travel and flights

Rusco International	222 Seven Sisters Road, London N4 3NX
Easy Jet	www.easyjet.com
Cheap Flights	www.cheapflights.co.uk
	www. easyvalue.com
Thomas Cook	www.thomascook.co.uk
Ebookers (a travel portal)	www.ebookers.com

Taxation

Inland Revenue	Fitzroy House, PO Box 46, Nottingham NG2 1BD

Information websites

Lonely Planet	www.lonelyplanet.com
Foreign Office Travel Advice	www.fco.gov.uk/travel
British Airways Authority	www.baa.co.uk

Appendix 10
Further reading

AA Essential Food and Drink Spain: (AA): Living to eat

AA Essential Spanish Phrase Book: (AA): Common sense phrases

AA Touring Spain: (AA): An excellent guide to touring in Spain

Andalucia Handbook: Rowland Mead (Footprint): A bible for Southern Spain

Cider with Rosie: Laurie Lee (Penguin): A classic

Como se dice...? : Paul Newbury (Hodder & Stoughton): Spanish vocabulary

Cooking in Spain: Janet Mendal (Santana): The essential cooking book for Spain

Culture Shock: Graff (Kuperard): A guide to Spanish customs and etiquettes

Death in the Afternoon: Hemingway (Grafton): His famous look at bullfighting

Driving Over Lemons: Stewart (Sort of Book) : An optimist in Andalucia

Eyewitness Spain: (Dorling and Kindsley): The best travel guide about Spain

Floyd on Spain: Keith Floyd (Michael Joseph): One dashing cook

Franco: Preston (Harper Collins): A definitive biography.

Internet Rough Guide: Angus Kennedy (Rough Guides): To keep in touch with home

Jogging around Majorca: West (black Swan): A 1920s travel book

La Rioja and its Wines: Scarborough (Survival Books): Excellent reading for lovers of wine

Living and Working in Spain: (ECA International): Demographics from the HSBC

Living in Spain: (Belvins and Franks): Financial affairs for residents

Nord Riley's Spain: (Santana): The life of a humorous wanderer

Spanish Lessons: Derek Lambert (Embury): Beginning a new life in Spain – a bestseller

Spanish Wines: Jan Read (Mitchell Beazley): A good wine guide

Suenos World Spanish: (BBC): Multi media course for beginners in Spanish

Sunflower Landscapes: (Sunflower Books): Three walking guides

Tapas and more great dishes from Spain: Janet Mendal (Santana): Spain's bar food

The New Spaniards: Hooper (Penguin): Life after Franco

The Spanish Civil War: Gabriel Ranzato (Windrush): A century in focus

The Spanish Property Guide: David Searl (Santana) : A detailed legal approach

The Spanish Tragedy: Carr (Phoenix): The civil war in perspective

Viva Espana: (BBC): Beginners' language course

Walking in Andalucia: Watts (Santana): Walking routes in national parks

We are in Hospital: Alicante University / Cam Bank: One for the bookshelf

Appendix 11
Common questions

What are the additional costs incurred when buying a new home?
It is wise to allow 10 per cent of the purchase value to cover the costs of conveyancing and taxes.

How much does it cost to run a home?
About 3,000 Euros per year, covering electricity, water, telephone, property insurance, local taxes and community charges.

Tell me about medical facilities.
Hospitals tend to be new. Doctors, dentists and medical centres are well advertised. They are staffed by highly qualified Spaniards and some northern Europeans. Many drugs are available without prescription from chemists who offer good advice. Non residents can claim free treatment by the use of form E11 available in most European countries. Residents below retirement age should take out a private health insurance at about 800 Euros per year. Residents over retirement age, or disabled, are entitled to free health care by entering the Spanish health system.

What are the main advantages and disadvantages of moving to Spain?
Spain offers an excellent climate, low cost of living, good healthy food and drink and a relaxed life style. Some of the disadvantages include a high petty crime rate and lots of 'red tape'.

Is the culture different?

Yes. Family ties are very strong. Drinking plenty of wine and eating late at night are differences. Café life, fiestas, flamenco and bull fighting are the traditional romantic values of Spain. An excellent climate leads to many outdoor activities.

There are many hypermarkets, but few departmental stores outside the large cities. Small family run shops are plentiful, making the shopping experience totally different.

Do we need a solicitor and fiscal representative?

Most definitely yes to both. An *abogado* is someone who can complete the legal process of buying a house and offer good advice. Fiscal representation is best obtained from a *gestor*, who is also highly qualified, dealing with residency, taxation and administrative matters.

What are we looking for in an estate agent?

Initially someone who can offer a wide range of properties in the area of your choice. A good agent will also be a member of a professional organisation.

What happens if the builder goes bankrupt?

Builders should have an insurance policy to protect their customers against this possibility. Please check.

Are sporting facilities plentiful?

The countryside and sea provide a natural backdrop for all sporting activities of which golf, bowling, tennis and walking are the most popular. For those people not interested in sport, social clubs exist for almost every type of activity.

Any myths?

Yes, one seems to constantly crop up. Upon death the Spanish Government do not reclaim your property. Just do the normal thing. Make out a Spanish will for Spanish assets.

Appendix 12
Useful phrases

Greetings

Hello	*Hola*
Good morning	*Buenos dias*
Good afternoon/evening	*Buenas tardes*
Good evening/night	*Buenas noches*
How are you?	*Que tal?*
Fine, how are you?	*Muy bien, y usted?*
See you later	*Hasta luego*
See you tomorrow	*Hasta mañana*
Goodbye	*Adios*

Useful words

Sorry	*Perdon*
Please	*Por favor*
Thank you	*Gracias*
You're welcome	*De nada*
It does not matter	*No importa*
Of course	*Claro*
Yes	*Si*
No	*No*
Sir	*Senor*
Madam	*Senora*

Questions

Where's the station?	*Donde esta la estacion?*
Where are the shoes?	*Donde esta los zapatos?*
Where is the hotel Melia Alicante?	*Donde esta el hotel Melia Alicante?*
How much is that?	*Cuanto es?*

Again

Pardon?	*Como?*
I do not understand	*No comprendo*
I do not know	*No se*
How do you write it?	*Como se escribe?*

People

My name is...	*Me llamo...*
What's your name?	*Como se llama?*
I'm Miss Pamela Smith	*Soy la senorita Pamela Smith*
Where are you from?	*De donde es usted?*
I'm from Ireland	*Soy de Irelanda*
What do you do?	*En que trabaja?*
I'm a nurse	*Soy enfermera*
I speak a little Spanish	*Hablo un poco Espanol*
Are you here on holiday?	*Esta usted aqui de vacaciones?*
Yes. I am here for a week	*Si. Paso una semana aqui*

Time

What time is it?	*Que hora es?*
It's one o'clock	*Es la una*
It's two/three/four o'clock	*Son las dos/ tres/ quatro*
It's half past three in the afternoon	*Son las tres y media de la tarde*
It's quarter to eleven at night	*Son las once menos cuarto de la noche*
What time do you open?	*A que hora abren?*
What time do you close?	*A que hora cierran?*

Colours

black	negro	orange	naranja
blue	azul	red	rojo
brown	marron	white	blanco
green	verde	yellow	amarillo

Numbers

0	cero	80	ochenta
1	un/una/uno	90	noventa
2	dos	100	cien
3	tres	101	ciento uno
4	cuarto	110	ciento diez
5	cinco	200	doscientos
6	seis	300	trescientos
7	siete	400	quatrocientos
8	ocho	500	quinientos
9	nueve	600	seiscientos
10	diez	700	setecientos
11	once	800	ochocientos
12	doce	900	novecientos
13	trece	1.000	mil
14	catorce	2.000	dos mil
15	quince	3.000	tres mil
16	dieciseis	1.000.000	una million
17	diecisiete		
18	dieciocho		
19	diecinueve		
20	viente		
21	vientiuno		
22	vientidos		
23	vientitres		
24	vienticuatro		
25	vienticinco		
26	vientiseis		
27	vientisiete		
28	vientiocho		
29	vientinueve		
30	treinta		
40	cuarenta		
50	cincuenta		
60	sesenta		
70	setenta		

Days

Monday	lunes	Saturday	sabado
Tuesday	martes	Sunday	domingo
Wednesday	miercoles	today	hoy
Thursday	jueves	yesterday	ayer
Friday	viernes		

Months

January	enero	July	julio
February	febrero	August	agosto
March	marzo	September	septiembre
April	abril	October	octubre
May	mayo	November	noviembre
June	juno	December	diciembre

Seasons

spring	la primavera	summer	el verano
autumn	el otono	winter	el invierno

The home

house	la casa
flat	la piso
room	la habitacion
living room	el salon
dining room	el comedor
kitchen	la cocina
bathroom	el bano
bedroom	el dormitorio
sofa	un sofa
chair	una silla
bed	una cama
table	una mesa

Index

Abogado, 77, 105, 119, 138
Accidents, 176
Additional buying costs, 103
Addresses, 179
Advertisements, 54
Agent's Agreement, 91
Almeria, 40
Andalucian, 21, 38
Apartment, 59
Aragon, 36
Architect, 135
Arts, 167
Autumn, 31

Balearics, 44
Bank, 79, 121
Bankruptcy Insurance Policy, 73
Barcelona, 35
Basque Country, 34
Black Money, 106
Bogus Agents, 76
Boredom, 190
Bowling, 186
Builder, 71
Building alterations, 98
Building Specification, 58
Bull fighting, 165
Bull running, 165

Canary Islands, 45
Capital Gains Tax, 158

Car, 149, 177
Car Hire, 115
Car Inspection, 149
Car Insurance, 178
Car Registration, 149
Catalonia, 36
Certificado Final de la Direccion de la Obra, 96
Climate, 18
Clothing, 171
Commissions, 74–75
Community Charges, 95
Community property, 63
Contract, 94, 136 -137
Corner properties, 60
Cost of Living, 20
Costa Blanca, 37
Costa Brava, 36
Costa de Azahar, 37
Costa de la Luz, 41
Costa del Sol, 40
Costa Dorada, 36
Crime, 22
Culture, 162

Debts, 85
Deposits, 102
Detached houses, 60
Direction, 65
Do It Yourself, 133
Driving Licence, 148

E-Commerce, 53, 116, 141
Economy, 28
Escritura, 84, 97
Estate Agents, 52, 73
Euro, 81

Family, 163
Fast track conveyance, 125–128
Fiestas, 164
Final payment, 122
Financial Advisor, 152
Fiscal Identification Number, 120
Fishing, 186
Flamenco, 165
Flights, 115
Food, 33, 34, 38, 42, 44,166
Furnishings, 107
Furniture purchase, 124
Furniture removal, 114

Galicia, 33
Garden, 67
Gestor, 85, 144
Gibraltar, 41
Golden rules, 87
Golf, 185
Gyms, 187

Health System, 150
Heating and Air Conditioning, 66
Hiking, 186
Hyper Markets, 170
History, 23
Holiday homes, 190
Holidays, 17, 51
House names, 57
House plan, 91

IBI, 146

Income Tax, 157
Inheritance Tax, 159
Inheritance Trusts, 155
Inmobiliaria, 52
Inspection flight, 50
Insurance, 96
International Property Companies, 51
Investment, 16, 153–154

La Rioja, 34
Landlord, 143
Language, 27
Learning Spanish, 111
Leisure, 182–185
Letting, 113
Licencia de Primera Occupacion, 96
Linked houses, 59

Terraced houses, 59
Town houses, 59
Living by the sea, 64
Living in the country, 65

Madrid, 43
Main cities, 28
Major house faults, 118
Mañana, 23
Marbella, 40
Medical facilities, 22
Mercado central, 172
Minor house faults, 119
Modern Spain, 25
Moorish cities, 42
Mortgage, 82
Moving in, 117
Murcia, 37

Names, 179
Navarra, 34
New property, 64
Newspapers, 47, 181
Non-Resident's Certificate, 82
Nota Simple, 93
Notario, 84, 123
Notary fees, 105

Offshore banking, 80
Olive oil, 172
Open-air markets, 171
Opera, 167

Padron, 146
Pensions, 153
People, 21, 28
Perceptions, 16
Pets, 112
Picos de Europa, 34
Planning Department, 134
Plot, 91
Plus Valia Tax, 104
Police, 182
Population, 27
Position, 67
Postal service, 178
Power of Attorney, 78
Problems, 86
Property descriptions, 57
Property exemption, 160
Property exhibitions, 48
Property prices, 101
Property Registry, 105
Pros and cons, 18
Pueblos Blancos, 42
Pyrenees, 34

Radio, 180

Red tape, 23
Reformed houses, 131
Registro de la Propiedad, 98
Religion, 163
Renovated houses, 131
Rental, 51, 140, 142
Resale house conveyancing,
    129–131
Resale property, 64
Residencia, 147
Retirement, 190
Road Tax, 148
Roads, 175
Running costs, 108
Running, 187

Security, 66
Selecting a Bank, 80
Sevilla, 39
Spanish language, 110
Sports Federations, 187
Spring, 30
Stage payments, 102
Stamp Duty, 104
Summer, 30
Swimming pool, 67

Tabac, 172
Tapas, 166
Tax deposit, 106
Taxation, 155
Telephone, 181
Television, 180
Tennis, 187
Tiendas, 169
Timeshare, 139
Today's Spain, 26
Tolerance, 190
Torrevieja, 37

Traditional homes, 62
Transfer Tax and IVA, 104

Urbanizations, 62

Valencia, 37
Vehicle entrances, 150

Wealth Tax, 159
Who buys what, 16, 69
Wills, 150
Wine, 172
Winter, 31
Women residents, 190

Golf   £128,000

For
Pool all year around.
large balcony.
well kept grounds
large appt.

Against
- distance from
  beach;
- no rest. in walk
  distance.

Bruno.   £136.000.

For

Beach location
access to bar/rest.
Supermarket in summer.
well kept gardens.
pool summer.

Agent
Pool closed
         winter.
small booking
price